TRUE BEAR TALES

TRUE STORIES FROM MICHIGAN'S UPPER PENINSULA

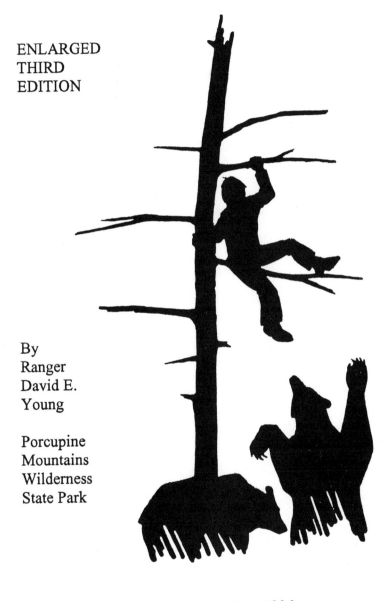

ENLARGED
THIRD
EDITION

By
Ranger
David E.
Young

Porcupine
Mountains
Wilderness
State Park

GOLDEN OAK BOOKS   1996

Published   1996

By

Golden Oak Books
605 Michigan Street
Ontonagon, Michigan 49953
(906) 884-2961

Enlarged Third Edition

ISBN 0-9623664-4-7

Printed in the United States of America

TABLE OF CONTENTS

PART I: TRUE BEAR TALES

PART II: NEW BEAR TALES

PART III: THE THIRD EDITION UPDATE

INTRODUCTION

This book is intended for anyone who wants an informative and entertaining collection of true black bear stories and general information about bears. It is especially directed towards those who come to the north woods to backpack and camp so they will know what to expect from the local bruins. Most of the incidents described in this book took place in or near Porcupine Mountains Wilderness State Park in the Western Upper Peninsula of Michigan. Many others occurred in the Copper Harbor / Fort Wilkins State Park area, also in the Western Upper Peninsula of Michigan. There are a couple stories which originated in Great Smoky Mountains National Park.

There are several specific reasons for the writing of this book. One was a hope that by providing factual information to outdoor enthusiasts about actual bear incidents, future problems with bears could be reduced or eliminated. Another had to do with the fact that a great part of the information in this book was never recorded anywhere else. It is preserved only in the memories of those who were involved in the incidents, or who investigated them at the time they occurred. Still another relates directly to the previous reason: The author was in the particularly fortunate situation to be aware of many of the incidents described. In some cases he was involved in the incidents. In others he was provided first hand accounts by fellow park employees and friends who were involved.

The author has purposefully presented most of the bear incidents in the collection from a humorous point of view, which is even reflected in the selection of the story titles. There is no reason why we should not look back and laugh at the various predicaments campers got themselves into in the past. However, everyone should be well aware that the people who were involved in these bear encounters were not amused in the least at the time the incidents were occurring. Yet there are very good reasons for presenting these stories with a chuckle. Readers will be more likely to read the stories if they are entertained by them. The chances that they will understand how and why the incidents happened will be increased. The end result will hopefully be that they are able to avoid future bear related problems while camping, hiking or engaged in other outdoor activities.

As readers of the first edition will quickly see, there has been no letup of bear activity at either Porcupine Mountains or Copper Harbor since the first edition of True Bear Tales was prepared in the spring of 1987. At the Porkies, it turns out in retrospect (hindsight always being 20/20) that the summers of 1988 and 1989 were exceptionally bad bear problem years. At Copper Harbor, the dump was closed during the 1990-1991 winter. It was expected that there would be increased bear problems around Copper Harbor as a result in the summer of 1991 and there were.

For those who have read the second edition, this third edition will clearly demonstrate that the trend towards more bear and human conflicts has continued. 1992 was a very unusual year in that many bears went to the towns for food, and 1994 was a record year for bear conflicts with backpackers at Porcupine Mountains Wilderness State Park. Hopefully, as new ideas in the form of bear proof food and trash containers catch on, this undesirable trend can be reversed.

ACKNOWLEDGMENTS

Special thanks are due to award winning nature photographer Dan Urbanski of Silver City, Michigan for the cover photograph on this edition of True Bear Tales.

Special thanks also go to Michael B. Rafferty, long time Porcupine Mountains Wilderness State Park Ranger, for the title page drawing (which was the cover illustration on the first edition of True Bear Tales).

The author wishes to thank all those staff members of Porcupine Mountains Wilderness State Park and Fort Wilkins State Park who shared their bear experiences with him. Their names will be found throughout the book.

He also wishes to thank his wife, Arlene, for, once again, tirelessly going over the manuscripts trying to make his writing comprehensible.

The author has tried to keep all accounts based upon factual and reliable sources, and assumes full responsibility if there are any shortcomings in that respect. Readers should be aware that most of this volume was written mainly from memory. The names in this book are the actual names of persons involved when known. Some names are fictitious because the real names are not known. The victims of a few incidents are left anonymous to spare them any embarrassment.

BEAR IN MIND

GENERAL BLACK BEAR INFORMATION

The following general information about black bears is provided so that readers will have a better understanding of these remarkable creatures.

NATURAL HISTORY

The forested areas of Michigan's Upper Peninsula are prime black bear habitat. A square mile of forest land will support a small bear. A more normal density for bears would be one bear for every 2 to 3 square miles of appropriate habitat. Bears do not respect artificial boundaries of course, and they do wander about somewhat, so the concept of a Park population of black bears is not particularly relevant to the bears. However, tourists are very fond of asking how many bears there are in the Porcupine Mountains Wilderness State Park (the Porkies), so for them the information is very much sought after. The Porkies covers about 60,000 acres or about 93 square miles. Thus, the area of the Porkies and the normal density of bears would result in an estimated population of around 30 bears for the Park. Note that bears are not migrating animals. They generally maintain territories within which they live. The territories may be quite large (up to four times the area of the Park) and often overlap other bears' territories.

The author believes that this estimate of the black bear population of the Porkies is reasonable. Factors influencing the numbers of bears include the normal demise of bears from old age and disease. There are seasonal variables affecting the number of bears. Newborn cubs increase the population upon their birth during the winter months. However, the population may decrease due to deaths of unhealthy bears which do not survive the winter hibernation. Also, the population is decreased during the fall hunting season, and may also be decreased during the summer if certain problem and fearless bears get out of hand and have to be removed or destroyed.

Bears may be active at any time of day. Except for during the mating season in late June and July, when the males and females are together for mating, and for sows with cubs, bears are generally solitary animals. Females reach maturity during their third year. Females normally have cubs every other year during hibernation. The normal number of cubs is two, although from one to four cubs are possible. The cubs stay with their mother and are taught and protected by her until their second summer. Then the sow leaves them on their own and mates again. Black bear may live to be 20 to 30 years old.

Do not be misled by the bulky and sluggish looks of a black bear. They can easily outrun any man, and unless exceptionally fat, they can climb trees faster than most people can run on the ground. Bears at the end of their first summer would normally weigh between 45 and 65 pounds, and older bears up to 400 pounds and more. Most bears are between 100 and 250 pounds. Larger ones are not common.

Bears retire into dens for hibernation during the coldest months, generally while the ground is frozen and there is snow cover. The main reason for hibernation in bears is the lack of food during the cold months. Bears are not true hibernators since their body temperatures do not significantly drop during their long winter sleep when they live off the fat deposits which they have built up during the warmer months.

A den may be a hollow under a tree stump, a cave, an excavated hole in a bank or hillside, or simply a hollow beside a rock. Bears sometimes do a lot of work hauling weeds into dens for a mat. Other bears are more lazy and simply lay down and go to sleep on the ground.

BEAR BEHAVIOR TOWARDS HUMANS

A wild black bear's normal inclination when people are nearby is to leave the area. It is suggested that hikers always let a black bear know of the hikers' presence. One method is for hikers to wear bells. The purpose is to prevent the bear from being unnecessarily startled, and to allow it to follow its natural proclivity to leave. Hikers should avoid situations where they might get quite close to a bear and then accidentally surprise it. There are numerous stories of people who have accidentally come too close to bear cubs and have been "attacked" by the sow. Usually in such cases the sow charges the person and stops a few yards away while angrily growling, chomping and popping its mouth, and generally letting the person know it is not happy. If you are ever in this situation it is my recommendation that you do not move! Pretend you have seen Medusa and have turned to stone! Let the bear vent its anger, but stand your ground. The bear will eventually leave. Wait until it is completely out of sight and hearing distance, or you may be treated to a second breathtaking, heart pounding performance. You may also be forced into using Grecian Formula for your new grey hair!

There are situations where trail hikers may come upon a bear in the trail which does not seem to want to move even though the bear is well aware of them. In such a case, the bear may have cubs, food, or both nearby. It may not leave. Instead, it may stand its ground and be willing to fight over any intrusions. To avoid provoking a bear in such a situation, hikers should retreat back down the trail and wait for the bear to move on, or go well out around the bear and back onto the trail past the bear as long as there will be no possibility of getting lost.

Black bears normally eat plants, fruits, berries, nuts, roots, fish, small animals, insects, honey and carrion. They will also eat whatever else they can get that smells good to them, including garbage and campers' food. They have an exceptionally good sense of smell, and have been known to detect backpackers' food which was totally sealed in plastic.

In the Upper Peninsula of Michigan in the past, bears often gathered at dumps, usually marked as bear pits on the tourist maps, where they could pick through the garbage. This behavior is no longer possible because the last open dump, at Copper Harbor, was closed during the winter of 1990-1991. Prior to then, however, the dumps of the Upper Peninsula were a main attraction for the bears and the tourists who wanted to watch them.

Everyone has heard that it is best not to feed bears, but few people seem to know why. It is not to avoid upsetting the bears' stomachs. First, someone purposefully feeding a bear may run out of food prior to the bear running out of appetite. This will undoubtedly displease the bear and may be detrimental to the structural integrity of the person's body. Second, it causes bears to lose their fear of man. The less afraid they become, the more bold they become. They go through a stage where they are still afraid of humans but will search out camps to look for food. During this stage, we might refer to them as "friendly" bears.

Friendly bears eventually turn into terrible pests which are potentially very dangerous. We might refer to these as "fearless" bears. There is nothing quite so bad in the woods while you are camping as a 250 pound fearless bear wanting to share your meal. Remember, such bears are *not* tame; they are completely wild but without any fear of man.

Exactly how do friendly bears originate? Well, this is my explanation. Normal wild bears will often come into camps during the still of the night. If the camp is clean and the food inaccessible, the campers will probably never know a bear had been nearby. If the camp has dirty pans or any food lying around, the pans will get banged around and licked clean, and the food will be missing. If such a bear keeps finding easy and delicious meals near camps, he is very likely to return on subsequent nights.

Such a bear's habit of coming near camps rewards his behavior with good easy meals. Also, his habits are slowly changed to seeking out places where there are people rather than avoiding humans. After continued success at this method of obtaining food, the bear may switch from other, more difficult methods of food gathering to concentrating on relieving campers of their abundant and very tasty supplies. If this occurs, such a bear would fit my definition of "friendly". Some of the more practiced friendly bears can even get at the well hung food supplies of experienced backpackers.

There have been a few bears which lost so much of their fear of man that they would fit much better into the fearless category than the friendly one. One such bear would wander into camp at chow time, sit down a few feet away from the campers who were cooking, and stare at them. This cute little trick on the part of a large bear always has the desired effect - the campers decide to go for a walk, and the bear eats. Mmmmm, those campers have goooood foooood! Other bears have been less genteel. One walked up to a circle of cooking backpackers and squeezed between two of them to take the food right out of the pot! No unnecessary waiting around for a meal that time!

Some bears have been known to pull mock charges. They run towards packers on the trail. The packers drop the packs and run, and the bear leisurely tears apart their packs for the food. Why they call these mock charges I don't know. The bear was not after the people, it was after the packs with food in them. Since it got what it was after, I would say they were real charges. What would happen if the campers did not drop the packs? Why is it that I am asking that question instead of answering it? It's because I don't know the answer and have never known of anyone who has not dropped their pack and run in those situations. Bears which pull mock charges are truly fearless and can be very dangerous.

This book contains a number of fairly detailed accounts of bear incidents, along with information on the probable or possible causes of the trouble which occurred. The stories are not intended to scare anyone away from backpacking, hiking or camping. They are intended to inform hikers and campers of situations, actions, and practices to avoid in bear country.

For those planning to go hiking in Porcupine Mountains Wilderness State Park (the Porkies), it may be somewhat reassuring to know that all of the bears involved in any of the injury incidents were destroyed. Also, the Park does attempt to remove and relocate bears which are getting a bit too friendly before they become fearless pests. They are released in other areas where they will hopefully not have people contact problems. (NOTE: All problems with bears in Porcupine Mountains Wilderness State Park should be reported to a Ranger as soon as possible.)

One thing has saved the Porkies from many more and even worse bear incidents than those given in this collection. It is the early fall bear hunting season. During this hunting season fearless bears and friendly pest bears are much more likely to be taken by hunters than the "normal" wild bears for obvious reasons. At the end of every summer camping season most, if not all, of the developing pest bears are thus removed from the Park. However, the overall population of bears in the Park is not seriously reduced in the long run.

Considering the large number of people who visit and camp in the Park each year, the number of bear caused injuries has been miniscule. Hopefully, that number can be reduced to nothing if the campers become aware of the causes of such incidents. Before 1970, most bear problems occurred along roads, at picnic sites, or in campgrounds reached by car. During the 1970's, several factors resulted in a shift of bear problems into the Park's interior. One of these factors was a tremendous increase in the number of backpackers. There were many more people carrying food around with them on the trail system. A second factor was a shift to the use of plastic trash bags in the vehicle access campgrounds, and removal of trash baskets which had sat around with garbage in them most of the time. The plastic garbage bags are supposed to be kept inside a vehicle or trailer and placed in a garbage dumpster when filled. Thus they are not lying around outside for animals to get into. A third reason for the change was the abandonment of the old Porkies dumps, which resulted in the dump bears going elsewhere.

The author has noticed a trend the last few years to an increase in problems in the trash dumpster areas of big campgrounds and restaurants. This is believed to be due to changes in the methods and timing of collecting the trash. There is trash present, and therefore bears are after it. Boo Boo, a bear at Presque Isle in 1985, and a persistent 200 pound bear recently hanging around the Silver City / Union Bay area are examples of this.

FOOD HANDLING FOR CAMPERS

Backpackers, other campers and tourists unknowingly contribute to the formation of pest bears by their camping and food handling habits. Backpackers have and create the most problems because they are carrying their food supply around with them right out in the bears' bailywick. Other campers can usually keep their food in coolers either in their vehicles or trailers. Backpackers tend to concentrate their actual camping into certain relatively small areas of the Porkies - Mirror Lake, the Big and Little Carp rivermouth areas, near the shelters, and near certain cabins. Since a substantial part of the backpackers take no precautions with their food, and an even larger part take entirely inadequate precautions, the bears get quite a bit of food without even trying hard. Example: There was one case where boy scouts put 25 pounds of freeze dried food in, of all places, the crotch of a large tree! This was the equivalent of a formal invitation to dinner for bears.

The following list of precautions might be referred to as:
The Ten Commandments Of Backpacking In Black Bear Country

1. Never feed bears.
2. Never put food in your tent. Note that food to a bear would include such things as toothpaste, mouthwash, gum, cologne, cough drops, etc.
3. Hang all food up immediately when you get to your camping area.
4. Hang food well away from your tent site (not directly above your tent.)
5. Keep all gear and clothing free of food smell.
6. Cook well away from your tent.
7. Clean up immediately after meals.
8. Do not bury garbage, as bears will just dig it up. Plan your meals to avoid producing unnecessary garbage as much as possible, and plan on transporting the garbage out of the park and handling it just like food.
9. If a bear gets at your food, consider it his - he will!
10. Warn black bears of your presence.

Note that nine of these directly relate to food. It is the author's view that the vast majority of bear incidents are related to food (the camper's food, that is), and that almost every such incident could be avoided if every person was very careful and responsible with their food supply at all times while in the woods. Unfortunately, it is not at all likely that campers are going to change overnight, and therefore, it is very likely that there will be plenty of the common, everyday type of bear incidents described in this book occurring in the future.

FOOD HANGING METHODS

The above drawing illustrates two possible methods
of hanging food bags to keep them from bears.

One method illustrated is to toss a rope over a branch and tie off the rope to a sapling which is bent down to tie onto, and let up to keep the rope away from bears.

Another method is to balance two food bags, or one food bag and a rock, on either end of a line over the branch. The first to be pulled up must be over 20 feet high. Then the second is attached to the other end of the rope which should be as high as can be reached. This one is then pushed up with a stick until both ends are at a safe distance from the ground. To retrieve the food, a stick is utilized to catch one end and pull it down for removal.

Another method, not illustrated, is to run a rope between two branches and hang the food bag on a rope over that stretched rope. It can be tied off as in the first method, or can be balanced over the rope as in the second method. Other combinations of the above methods are also possible.

OTHER FOOD HANGING POINTERS

Hang food on the smallest branch which will support the food bag but will not support the weight of a bear.

Hang food sealed in plastic bags inside a special nylon sack carried solely for that purpose.

The food must be 12 to 15 feet or more above the ground, at least 6 feet from the trunk of the tree, and preferably 4 or 5 feet below the branch.

A second tie off rope over a different branch and tied to a different location may frustrate some especially agile bears. Several bears have been known to chew off branches to get food. If you run into one of these bears, your backpacking trip will probably be much shorter than you planned unless you are willing to fast the rest of it.

PART I: TRUE BEAR TALES

A Revision And Enlargement Of The First Edition

DOWN AND OUT IN PORCUPINE MOUNTAINS

Even though it may be very nice and sunny during the day in the month of October, it can also be pretty chilly, especially at night - often below freezing. I remember such an October day back in the mid 1970's when I got "stuck" in the park headquarters answering the phone and such because the secretary was not in that day. It was a normal, slow, boring and uneventful day until 10:05 a.m. when a man wearing baggy pants, a funny looking coat, and big floppy boots came limping into the office. I asked him if he was okay. He said "Yes, but I was attacked by a bear."

His name was Jim Clifton and here is his story: He had been backpacking alone, and had set up camp on top of Cloud Peak the previous afternoon. He was suddenly awakened in the middle of the night by grunting sounds and the clanging of his cooking set which was right outside his tent. It sounded like a large bear was tearing up his pack which was also sitting just outside his tent. He was very much awake now, and could clearly hear the bear chewing on his equipment and moving around the site. Suddenly, the tent lurched to one side - the bear must have run into a tent guy line. Then the bear hit another line, the tent pulling to that side. Next the bear, which sounded very large, bumped into the tent itself. Jim decided that this bear was going to not only chew up his equipment, but probably him as well.

This all happened so very quickly, Jim did not have time to make any real plans of what to do. When the bear bumped into the tent, Jim was so terrified that he bailed out the door and scrambled quickly away. The direction he was going was towards a cliff edge of the escarpment. He was scared out of his wits and running for his life. He went right to the cliff edge and down. This was most certainly not a conscious choice. It was pitch black outside, and he was without his absolutely essential prescription glasses. Besides, he was in his skivies and barefoot. On top of all this, it was cold outside - around 28 degrees. Of course none of these things concerned him very much until after he had climbed down the escarpment and had a little time to think about what was going on around him.

It is amazing that Jim was not injured in the dark while climbing down from Cloud Peak. He had quickly descended an area of alternating sheer drops and "stacks", or more gradual cuts in the rock face. Since he could not see anything, he had felt his way down. After pinching himself as he got off the steep area to make sure this was no dream, he realized the new predicament he was in. Fortunately he was familiar enough with the trail locations that he knew which general direction to head in order to reach his car. It was located about two and a half miles away at Lake of the Clouds Scenic Area.

Jim more or less had to feel his way to the west through the woods below the escarpment until he reached the Lake of the Clouds cabin area. He then climbed up a ravine towards the north which was the route of the old North Mirror Lake Trail. At the top of the hill he went west again up to the parking lot at the scenic viewing area where his car was. He was freezing, and his feet were so raw from the trek that he had to limp. When he got to his car, he could not get in. He felt around and found a rock to break the window with. Then he dug out some old clothes he had in the car, put them on, piled some others to cover himself, and went to sleep. The bear incident probably occurred around midnight. It took Jim around three hours to get to his car from his campsite.

He woke up about daybreak and limped down to the park headquarters since he had no car keys. Now, here he was in his old clothes trying to convince me that the bear attacked him. I was trying to reassure him that the bear was just tearing up his camp because he had left his food and dirty dishes lying around outside his tent. Jim wanted to retrieve his equipment and especially his glasses and car keys, but he did not want to go back to his campsite alone. Jerry Beck, a long time park employee gave Jim a ride back to his car and accompanied him to his campsite.

On the trip up to Cloud Peak, Jerry noticed several large bear droppings and commented that there appeared to be a big bear hanging around the area because of the fresh sign. Jim replied that there definitely were fresh droppings around because he had stepped in one last night which was *warm*. When they got to Jim's camp site, there was ample evidence of the bear's activity. Jim's equipment, his cookset, his tent, and everything had been destroyed by the bear's chewing and tearing. The bear spared none of his equipment. He was able to find everything except for his food, but almost everything bore the marks of the bear - claw and tooth marks. Clearly this large bear could have nabbed Jim in the cold night if it had the least desire to do so. It had Jim at every disadvantage - cold, blind and without any weapons or tools.

The most likely reason that this bear did such extensive damage to Jim's equipment was that Jim was not neat and clean with his food and utensils. He had left his pack and food just outside his tent. Also, his dirty pan and dishes were there, carelessly set aside to be cleaned up the following day. From this information we can deduce that Jim probably took little or no precautions whatsoever with his food supply, and that all of his equipment was saturated with unnecessary food smells. Perhaps it was a good thing that Jim had abandoned his camp when he did. Otherwise he might have had a fate similar to that which befell the young backpacker in the story entitled *All the Wrong Moves.*

GUESS WHO'S COMING TO DINNER

During 1975, 1976, and 1977 there was a large boar bear which inhabited the Mirror Lake area (let us refer to him as Bruno). This bear weighed in at around 250 pounds and was unintentionally kept well fed by all of the backpackers who visited this beautiful spot in the middle of the Porcupine Mountains. During the 1970's there were 25%-50% yearly increases in the number of backpacking camps at the park, so each year there was more and more food being carried around on the interior of the park. Some bears were learning about it and taking advantage of the fact. Bruno was one of those - a true master at getting backpackers' food.

On one occasion, an experienced backpacker who was thoroughly amazed by the bear's actions, told the author how the big bruin got his pack down from where it had been hung to keep it safe from bears. The packer had diligently hung it way out on a large branch so a bear could not just climb out and grab it. He had also raised it well off the ground so it could not be reached by a bear standing or jumping for it. In addition to all of this, the tree it was hung from was right on the edge of a 10 foot high solid rock face of the type very common around the north shore of the lake.

Bruno arrived uninvited and sized up the situation. He went up into the tree while the camper watched to see what he would do. After snorting around in the tree for a short while, the bear climbed out on the branch the food was hung from. The branch would support the

-19-

bear near the tree, but not as far out as the food bag was hung. Then the bear walked back and forth on the branch, and this got the pack swinging a little bit. It continued doing this until the pack was swinging back and forth a lot. Then Bruno climbed down the tree trunk to the point where the pack was swinging and took a one pawed grab at the pack as it swung in close. He couldn't quite hold it. The next time it swung in, Bruno jumped off the tree trunk onto the pack with both front paws, swung away from the tree like Tarzan, tearing the pack apart and down out of the tree. Bruno then proceeded with his feast. The backpacker had never seen anything like this feat before. The only thing that balanced his anger about losing his pack was that he had seen how the bear had done it.

This is a good place to mention that it is *not* a good idea to hang up food in a pack. If a bear is able to get at the food, as in the above case, the pack is most likely to be damaged or destroyed. Instead, it is a much better idea to carry a small nylon sack containing all food inside of plastic bags. Hang up only the nylon bag of food, leaving the pack itself open and empty on the ground. If park bears (which associate packs and food) come around, they can examine your pack without having to damage it. As long as your pack does not have food spilled on it, it should not be damaged utilizing this method.

Bruno, the Mirror Lake bear, was a "regular" in that the rangers received reports all summer long for several summers on how he got backpackers' food. Each year he became more proficient at getting the backpackers' food. He was big, partly because he was well fed. This made it possible for him to defend his territory and keep all other bears away from the area. The north shore of Mirror Lake was and is the single largest and most concentrated area of backpack camps in Porcupine Mountains Wilderness State Park. The rangers could never figure out why it was that the backpackers would go out into the woods to get away from it all, and yet the vast majority of them would crowd into camps at six different spots within the park. This makes it easier for bears to learn how to take advantage of them. It concentrates the food supply so bears don't have to travel as much for food once they learn how to get it.

During the third summer of Bruno's rule at Mirror Lake he developed another method which he used when he came across people who were in the process of handling or cooking food, or in the middle of a meal. There was less energy expended by Bruno with this method. No climbing or jumping was involved. Not only was this technique described to me several times by various backpackers to whom it had occurred, but also by Ranger Dave Peloso who observed such an incident from a hilltop about 50 yards away. As I said before, Bruno the bruin weighed in at around 250 pounds. What he would do is simply walk up in plain sight of whoever was cooking or eating and sit down about 10 or 15 feet away from them. Then he would just watch them. Just imagine this happening to you out in the woods. It undoubtedly scared something out of everyone it ever happened to. The result was always the same; the campers decided they would rather be somewhere else and they went there right away. This conveniently left the food all to Bruno.

Now that is what I call a pretty slick method of snitching food. I imagine that all of the campers this happened to were grateful to Bruno for taking their food instead of them. The bear got fat, and the campers had a first class wilderness experience which they could relate many times throughout the rest of their lives to their fortunate offspring.

Bruno was actually quite well behaved. Other than the people who ended up face to jowl with him, no one was actually worried about him hurting anyone. However, as with almost all bears which become attached to camper's food, this idylic situation could not go on forever. Sooner or later Bruno would cross over into "the fearless zone." There was a very fine imaginary line which separated the fearless zone bears from "friendly" nuisance bears. One was a "friendly" seeming pest which would keep his distance, while the other was a fearless and potentially dangerous pest which would not keep his distance.

IN THE STILL OF THE NIGHT

It was dark - very dark. There was no moon to see by. While the stars were very clear, there was no one to watch them at two in the morning. There was no sound, no breeze to whisper in the leaves or pine needles. Well, there was a slight soft snore from a leader of the Boy Scout troop. Everyone was fast asleep. They had arrived at Mirror Lake in fine weather after a three hour hike and were all very tired. It was as peaceful and quiet as could possibly be imagined in one's happiest dreams about one's vacation.

Suddenly there was a blood curdling scream!!! "EEEEEEEEeeeeeeee! Help! A BEAR, A BEAR! A BEAR, A BEAR!" Eyes jolted open, flashlights went on in ten different tents. The leader, heart pounding, scrambled out of his tent and over towards the commotion. A trembling twelve year old boy scout, his upper body sticking out from a pup tent, was spewing out words so fast they didn't make any sense at all.

"ItwasrightinhererighttherewithmeahugebearsniffingmyfaceandstinkyandI wokeupandwasscaredandscreamedandcouldn'tfindmylightanditranout."

English translation; "It was right in here with me. A huge bear sniffing my face and stinky. I woke up and was scared and screamed. I couldn't find my light, and it ran out."

Well, that's not your average "heard a noise and the bear got our food out of the tree in the night" story, eh? But it is what happened out at Mirror Lake in 1977.

That night while snooping around a Boy Scout Troop's camp, Bruno made a fatal error. He could smell something - something really good in one of the tents - a candy bar! He wasn't trying to hurt anyone, or even scare them, but as with humans, bears sometimes accomplish things entirely different than what they had intended. He very slowly and cautiously went into that pup tent and sniffed all the way in. Now imagine, if you will, a 250 pound boar blackbear in the middle of the night, sniffing around inside of a pup tent with a Boy Scout in it! A little crowded you might think.

Yes, this really happened. Yes, the Boy Scout did scream, more than once, and blood curdling screams to boot. Bruno couldn't get out of the tent fast enough. He had never had this happen to him before, and neither had the Boy Scout! Bruno disappeared into the night as everyone was jolted awake by the screaming. They all groped for their flashlights and apprehensively rushed to the source of the commotion. Fortunately, no one was hurt. Heart conditions may have been aggravated, and the leader's hair was undoubtedly more gray than a few minutes before, but everyone was okay. However, Bruno in his haste to be somewhere else as fast as possible had scratched the boy. Bruno was now considered to have entered the fearless zone. That signed Bruno's death warrant.

By now it was clear that Bruno had been getting much too close to people during his intimidating self invitations to dinner. It was evidently only a matter of time before something much worse might happen. The authorities decided to dispose of him. It was a relatively simple matter to locate the bear since he exclusively picked on campers at Mirror Lake.

Dave Peloso, one of the spotting rangers out looking for Bruno observed the bear come up and sit down across the camp stove from a young couple. The couple decided they needed to go for a walk. The ranger radioed for a nearby Conservation Officer who was to do the actual shooting. A few minutes after the couple left for their walk, Bruno was no more.

Now, before everyone starts berating the authorities for destroying Bruno, which was truly an unfortunate result, we should attempt to determine why a bear would become such a problem, and how such a situation might be avoided in the future. Clearly, Bruno was able to get almost any backpacker's food supply one way or another. But remember, Bruno had to start his camp raids sometime in the past when he was not very adept at it. It was very careless backpackers who unintentionally fed him and led him away from his safe natural food gathering ways into the ultimately destructive camp raiding behavior.

The author must say that on numerous occasions he and the other rangers at Porcupine Mountains Wilderness State Park have not only observed careless food handling practices on the part of backpackers, but have often had such practices described to us by the packers themselves when reporting bear incidents. As an example, in the summer of 1989 backpackers reported an incident along the Little Carp River to the author at the Porkies Visitor Center. They described a large bear in the woods across the river coming towards their camp. They decided it would be a good idea to throw some of their food towards the bear to save the rest. When asked how far the bear was away when they took this action, they replied about 100 yards! It is entirely possible that this bear was unaware of their presence until they started throwing food in its general direction. Needless to say, campers who value the lives of wildlife should never give or allow animals to get any food whatsoever.

ARMED AND DANGEROUS

In 1977, there was a bear which lived around the Correction Line Trail in Porcupine Mountains Wilderness State Park. This particular bear developed some very unusual and dangerous behavior patterns. The bear had learned to hunt for food in the backpackers' camps at two fairly busy camping spots - Mirror Lake and the Big Carp shelter area. During the first part of the summer, it was "hitting" the camps at the Big Carp shelter in the morning and at Mirror Lake in the evening. His behavior pattern changed in the middle of the summer, and he started hitting the camps at the reverse time of day - Mirror Lake in the morning and Big Carp in the evening.

One thing which this bear did regularly was pull mock charges on backpackers. Only one other bear ever did this in the Porkies as far as the author is aware. In a mock charge, the bear comes running full speed down the trail at the backpackers. This generally scares the daylights out of the packers, who drop everything and beat a hasty retreat. Thus the bear is left with the packs. Pretty neat, eh? This bear was a master of mock charging. It undoubtedly developed this skill in its travels back and forth between Mirror Lake and Big Carp shelter along the Correction Line Trail. In one particular case a couple reported losing two packs - one filled with only camera equipment. Both packs were dragged away off the trail by the bear never to be seen again. The backpackers made some searches later in the area for the equipment, but came up with nothing.

It is certain that this bear did not want the pack for its camera gear, only for any food it might contain. This case just demonstrates the extent to which bear learn to associate packs with food. Bear do not pass up food when they locate it in the woods. To a bear which learns to pick on backpackers, packs are just like some kind of food pod. As soon as a food pod is sighted, the bear takes it - one way or another. Bears usually locate these pack 'food pods' hanging in trees near where humans are camping, sometimes leaning against trees near camps, but always around or on humans. Some bears, this one included, discover that packs contain food. Once this happens, the bear is likely to search for camp sites since it associates them with people, people with packs and packs with food.

How a bear develops the mock charge behavior is not known for sure, but it is not something which most backpack loving bears learn to do. Therefore, it could either be a behavior which only certain bears learn due to a charcateristic in the particular bear's personality or to a rare sequence of events leading to learning it. Of course it is possible that both hypotheses are correct - certain fairly rare circumstances are required to occur and to involve a bear which is prone to aggressive behavior. One thing is for sure, the Correction Line Trail bear was *not* afraid of man, did develop the mock charge behavior, and had probably a better chance than most for run ins with packers since it traveled back and forth so much on that trail.

STAND BY ME

The author was told of a fairly humorous incident involving this bear by an occupant of the Mirror Lake 4 Bunk Cabin in 1977. That summer the backpackers were constantly running to the cabins seeking help in keeping their packs away from the Mirror Lake bear. Actually there were two bears, Bruno, and this very aggressive smaller one. On this occasion two young men ran yelling to the 4 bunk cabin that a bear had taken one of their packs, that they needed help, etc. Max, the cabin occupant, a gentleman of about 50 years old, gave them his advice: "Calm down! Ya don't have to be afraid of no bear! Ya see, bears are afraid of people - unless ya let them run all over ya. All ya have to do when ya see a bear is put yer hands on yer hips and stare right at im. He aint gonna come near ya when he knows yer not afraid of im."

Max, after stating his conceptions of bear behavior, asked what had happened. The two young men said they had stopped just west of the cabin, leaned their packs against one of the huge trees, and stepped over to the lakeshore about 15 feet away for a moment. When they turned around, a bear had grabbed one of the packs, and was proceeding to drag it up the hill away from the lake. Seeing this, the young men got really scared, started yelling and ran for help to the cabin. "There, ya see," Max said, "Ya wouldn't have had that happen if ya woulda stared im down. Come on, lets go get yer other pack."

They all walked back to the west about 50 yards where they found the other pack leaning undisturbed against the huge tree. The men showed Max where the bear had dragged the other pack up the hill, and Max stated again that bear were afraid of people and you could stare them down!

Just then, up pops this bear at the top of the hill. The guys pointed and yelled "Look, there it is now." Max spun around and sure enough, there he was. Max assured the young men again that it was easy to stare a bear down. Perhaps Max had seen it done in a movie? So, he put his hands on his hips and insisted that the others do so too. They all spread their legs, puffed up their chests and stared right at the bear. What Max didn't know, but was going to soon find out, was that this was a fearless schizoid park bear!

Well, the bear paused and sized up the situation - a luscious pack leaning against a tree - no need to even tear it down - and three men standing still looking at him and making no noise - sort of unusual. He was used to people making lots of noise to try and scare him away - banging pots and pans together and that sort of stuff. In fact, banging pots had sort of become music to his ears. After all, where there were pots, there was food! Well, as I said, he paused - maybe 20 or 30 seconds. That is quite a long time for such a situation; try counting it. And then, down the hill he came lickity split heading right for the pack. The guys held their formation until the bear was about half way, then they all scattered off to the east toward the cabin yelling just as had happened before.

The author asked Max why they didn't just grab the pack and take it back to the cabin when they had a chance. He said it was because he couldn't believe that a bear would come up to a man that was staring right at him. Well, remember this folks - a bear might very well come up to you even if you are staring straight at it - especially if you are between it and its cubs, its food, or the only exit!

Another unusual and very menacing behavior of this particular bear was its campground etiquette. It was quite successful at getting packs which campers had hung up. When it was not successful however, it appeared to be piqued. In every reported case around the Big Carp River shelter and Mirror Lake area where this bear was unsuccessful after trying to get a pack, it then went over to the campers' tent and damaged it. In one case it tore the tent down, in another it just jumped on the tent and knocked it down, and in two other cases it took a swipe at a side of the tents which cut long slits in them. In one of these last cases there happened to be a woman inside the tent at the time.

The case of the tent being torn down was graphically described to the author by one of the four campers, all of whom were noticeably upset, angry, and rather fearful. They had decided to leave immediately after this occurrence because of the strange behavior of this bear and its entire lack of fear. The tent involved was a rather expensive one and was brand new. The campers were experienced and there was no possibility of food smell on the tent. The bear tried for some time to get at the food, which had been hung very carefully from a large dead tree, but he had no success. After all of his attempts to get the food failed, he came down from the tree, went directly to the tent, and proceeded to tear it apart - then left.

The incident involving the tent with the lady inside resulted in attempts by the authorities to eliminate this bear. However, the timing of the bear's activities had changed which resulted in the inability to locate it during that season. After the authorities' attempts, this bear continued to hit camps and pull mock charges, but he no longer damaged tents, so further attempts to rid the park of him ceased. While this bear has been referred to above as a "he," the author believes that this bear was actually a sow which turned up the next season with four little cubs. This would explain why Bruno tolerated her in his territory at Mirror Lake. It is very possible that Bruno was a sire of her cubs. The following summer she became the worst problem bear the park ever had to deal with and was involved in the death of a camper.

SHE WAS THE TERROR OF THE PORKIES

In the summer of 1978 the first and only bear related fatality at Porcupine Mountains Wilderness State Park occurred. The bear involved was a sow with four cubs. A sow with four cubs in Michigan is quite rare - two is the normal number, and occasionally three. It is possible that this sow picked up a couple of cubs from another sow which died. The bear is believed to be the very same one which caused problems the previous season along the Correction Line Trail. Both bears were entirely fearless of man and were amazingly determined backpack stalkers.

Without any prior bear problems having been reported that season, the Park received word of a body having been found along the Lake Superior Trail during the second week of June. A male 19 year old camper, Mike Patterson, had been backpacking alone and apparently had some kind of run in with bears. While the autopsy indicated that his death was due to internal injuries (ruptured spleen and liver undoubtedly received in a fall from a tree), it is known for sure that a bear was involved and probably was responsible for the fall from the tree. According to other rangers who went to the scene, the body was lying near the base of a dead fir or spruce tree. There were two bite wounds on the body - one on the calf and one on the buttocks.

No one knows what happened out on the Lake Superior Trail as there were no witnesses. There were numerous bears tracks all around the camp site - tracks of large and of many small bears. There was clear evidence that a bear had climbed the fir tree from which the hiker had clearly fallen. There were broken branches down one entire side of the tree, clear sign of black fur on branches, and claw marks up into the tree.

Now, while no one knows what did happen in this case for sure, let us speculate on some possibilities. We know that black bears generally do not attack humans. We know that this has occurred sometimes, and that when it has occurred it usually involved protective behavior - protection of cubs or protection of a food supply. There have been a few documented cases (in other areas) where black bears have attacked humans as a food source. In this case the bear obviously did not consider the man as a food source because, even though he had been bitten, there was no evidence that the bear tried to eat him. The bear clearly had the opportunity to do so.

The most logical explanation for what happened in this case is what could be described as defensive attack behavior. Possibly it involved the cubs, possibly the backpacker's food supply, or maybe both. We do know that Mike had left his camp to wash a shirt. His shirt was found drying on bushes beside Lake Superior about 100 yards from camp. His knife was found on the ground near the tree he fell out of. Suppose Mike came back from washing his shirt, found mama in his camp and tried to scare her away from his gear. Mama decided to chase him away, so he ran to a tree and started climbing, but mama followed him right up. Or maybe he tried to chase a cub away from his gear and mama treed him all the way up. There is the possibility that the cubs were in the tree which Mike climbed or in another one nearby. It is also possible that he climbed the tree all on his own just because he saw a bear, fell out of it injuring himself fatally, and that the bear bit him then in some kind of protective reaction.

No one will ever know for sure what happened, but there is one thing we do know for sure. Your food is not worth your life. This does not mean that one should drop or throw food to bears just because one sees a bear. That would teach bears to expect food from people. If they never got any food from humans, they would not develop a taste for such food. Every one of the bears which became problems in the Porkies learned their behavior because of the sloppy food handling practices of *some* campers. If every backpacker always took reasonable precautions with their food, bears could not learn to be bandits.

Taking reasonable precautions means to immediately hang the food up properly after selecting a camp; then remove and use what is needed from the supply and immediately rehang the rest. There is a tendency among some folks in the woods to throw all or some of their food to a bear upon sighting one. Another common action of backpackers is to quit taking precautions if they do not happen to have problems on their first couple of nights out in the woods. This is how bears become problems. I am not suggesting that during a mock charge one should not drop a pack. I don't know what would happen if the pack is not dropped. It probably depends upon the bear. But I do suggest never to purposely feed any bear, and never to drop equipment just because you happen to see a bear.

Reports started pouring in from the Lake Superior Trail about an aggressive sow with four little cubs the day after the body was found. The backpackers reported fascinating stories of how this sow would march into camp and take over all packs in sight. Anyone who tried to recover their pack had this mama bear there instantly to contend with. She clearly functioned on the premise that possession is nine tenths of the law. Mama needed all the food she could get to keep her offspring fed. She usually didn't let any packs slip away from her. There was only one that the author has heard of. The following story was related by the leader of a youth group consisting of about eighteen people.

After having selected a camping area near the mouth of the Big Carp River, the members of the youth group were all setting up their equipment. Their packs were strewn all around on the ground and up against tree trunks. Suddenly, this fairly good sized bear came into camp followed by four little ones. The big bear would not let anyone near a pack. It proceeded to tear packs apart with little effort since none had been hung up yet.

One of the campers decided he was not going to let the bear damage his pack because he had it half full of camera gear. He grabbed his pack, which was on the end of the camp closer to the river and further away from the bear. He took off with it as fast as he could across the bridge near the rivermouth. Mama bear noticed this pretty quickly and tore out after the 'thief'. She took off at an angle into the rivermouth to cut off the poor guy. Once into the river, however, she was distracted by the myriads of redhorse suckers which literally covered the bottom. She grabbed one of these and seemingly forgot about the guy fleeing with his backpack. She meandered back and destroyed the rest of the packs. But no one else was so hardy as to attempt to steal back their pack from her. And, it may be proper to observe here that the packer who did get away with his pack was probably darned lucky!

There were many other reports of this bear invading camps, commandeering all packs and leaving nothing for the poor packers who carried the food into the park. Many, many camps left early that season - they had to, because they had no food to eat. It did not take a genius to figure out which particular bear was involved in the death of the backpacker after the sudden influx of reports concerning this extremely aggressive and fearless bear with four cubs.

Since the authorities were certain which bear was involved in this incident, an attempt was made to destroy her. A prime spot along the Lake Superior Trail was selected in the middle of the area where this bear had been hitting camps. It was decided to try to lure the bear to this particular spot by baiting it. One of the park rangers, Dave Peloso, was a trapper who had prepared bait for his trap lines. Trappers are secretive sorts who take all kinds of precautions to hide their own smell, and they prepare some pretty bitter brews to attract animals and cover the trapper's scent.

The bait consisted of rotten fish kept in a bottle for who knows how many years. This stuff smelled so bad that the rangers could barely stand to set it out. All during the afternoon and evening while they hid waiting upwind from the baited area for their quarry to appear, they witnessed a succession of hikers going by on the trail who were visibly stunned by the odor. After the first whiff, they would start looking around on the ground. Then after a couple more steps, they would stop and look at the bottoms of their boots. This was potent bait. Suddenly a bear appeared. It was a small bear without cubs, not the one being sought. It came in and went straight for the bait. Mean mama and cubs did not appear, however. She had left the Lake Superior Trail. But she was destined to cause other problems, and to go out with a bang.

It was not long, just a few days, before rangers found out where the bear had moved to. On June 29, word came in of a bear problem down by the North Mirror Lake Trail bridge. Three female backpackers who were traveling north on the North Mirror Lake Trail were forced to drop their packs by the sow with four cubs a few yards before reaching the bridge. The girls ran off into the woods while the bear proceeded to tear the packs apart and eat all the food. Since mama bear was at the south end of the bridge, the girls were thus stranded in the woods on that side of the bridge. The stranded gals stayed out in the woods to the south of the bridge and started yelling for help - "HELP, BEAR, HELP."

Now this particular location is the busiest spot in Porcupine Mountains Wilderness State Park. It is directly below the famous main overlook at Lake of the Clouds Scenic Area. This just happened to be a very nice day, and there were many people around the lookout area above the bridge. Naturally, this yelling about bear in the woods attracted a lot of attention, and rather than leaving after seeing the sights, most people were sticking around to see what was happening with the bear problem down below. Quite a crowd was developing at the overlook.

The situation was quickly reported, and ranger Jim Richardson was dispatched to investigate. Jim took a two way radio and a power megaphone with him to the area. He could hear the yells for help from the other side of the river as he neared the north end of the bridge. When he was about a hundred yards from the bridge, a man came walking towards him from that direction. Jim questioned him on how much further down the trail the bear was, and the man indicated it was about a mile away. So Jim took off jogging and tramped across the bridge full speed, probably sounding like a troop of marines.

As he sped off the end of the bridge after just being told it was a mile to the bear, he was amazed to see Mean Mama Bear leaning against a tree on the side of the trail only 30 feet away. He screeched to a halt and started to pale while the sow welcomed him with a swipe of its paw and really hefty, nasty growl. This bear did not like someone running up to her like that, and she was not about to be scared away by the likes of Jim. Her four cubs were nearby. By now Jim was stopped, and his complexion had turned several shades lighter than normal. He was beginning to back off while assessing his options which were few. Here Jim was, 20 or so feet from the nastiest bear any of the park staff had ever heard about, having almost run into it, and he had no weapon. So he whipped up his megaphone which was set on high and gave the bear a good blast of police siren at close range. Fortunately, mama turned and started up the yellow birch tree right next to her, probably because the sound was so loud and entirely new to her. Jim backed away, then ran back across the bridge as fast as he could go. He had already decided that he was jumping into the river if mama followed him. At the north end of the bridge, after assuring himself he was not being followed, he megaphoned the girls to stay put and radioed for reinforcements.

Meanwhile, up above at the overlook the crowd of onlookers was increasing in size, and so was the story of what was going on down below. Reinforcements arrived with more radios and firearms. Jim Richardson and Jim Cooper, the Park Naturalist, then proceeded to solve the problem. The bear was approached much more quietly this time than last. They slowly made their way around the bear from the bridge end. One would cover the bear with his firearm while the other moved about 15 feet, then they would switch roles. After reaching the girls, the rangers escorted them back to safety by retracing their steps back around Mean Mama and onto the bridge. Once again they alternated covering the bear and moving forward. After the girls were on the safe side of the bridge, they went back to dispose of the bear which had remained on the lower trunk of the yellow birch tree near the torn up packs ever since Jim had startled her with the megaphone.

And what a bear she was - a nasty disposition, aggressive, fearless, would not take no for an answer when it came to getting hiker's packs - and now she was putting herself into a position which could not be overlooked without action. And so, with a huge crowd of onlookers from up above on the overlook, the rangers prepared to shoot Mean Mama to bring peace and security back for the trailside campers of the Porkies. Just as they were taking aim on the bruin, a man came out of nowhere and complained about what they were going to do. While Jim Richardson covered the bear, Jim Cooper explained the situation to the man - that the bear had been involved in a backpacker's death, and that it had just caused a major problem right where they were. They then told the man not to interfere in their work and to leave, which he did. They then shot Mean Mama.

Ever since Jim had almost run into the bear, the four cubs had been up in the top of a large ash tree about fifty yards away. There was some debate now about whether they would starve and should therefore be destroyed or not. The man who had tried to stop them from shooting the bear before returned and convinced them that the cubs should be left alone regardless of whether they would starve or not. Approximately an hour after the bear was shot, the author helped haul the carcass of Mean Mama off the trail back into the woods. The four cubs were still up in the top of the ash tree where they were left to fend for themselves. Thus ended The Terror of the Porkies.

Since this incident was viewed by such a large number of park visitors, news reports concerning it were published all around the midwest. Shortly afterwards, the park started receiving hate mail from persons who were upset that the bear had been destroyed. I think it safe to say that none of the personnel at Porcupine Mountains Wilderness State Park ever got any enjoyment from having had to destroy a bear. We would all much rather have the users of the park be much more careful about their food so that the bears can mature without becoming dangerous pests, which the rangers then have to deal with.

TO BE HERE OR NOT TO BE HERE, THAT IS THE QUESTION

In 1971, I worked as a seasonal employee at Fort Wilkins State Park near Copper Harbor, Michigan. I was to live in a tent behind the office in the park's service area. My tent was about ten feet from the back of the garage and right on the edge of the woods. Since it was so close to the service garage, I had an extension cord run into the tent for a tiny refrigerator and hot plate. There was a bathroom in the garage, thus the only thing I lacked was a kitchen sink.

The first day when I came "home" to my tent from work I got quite a surprise. There were two small bears in the front of the service garage. When I came out the back door which was right in front of my tent, there was a sow and a cub just clearing the back corner of the garage. Altogether there were four bears wandering around the service area - a sow with three cubs. They were not yet near my tent but were slowly meandering around that way. They were not aware of my presence yet, so I decided that I must attempt to scare them away by surprising them. First I located all the bears, then prepared a secure getaway - the back door into the garage and a second door from there into another room. Leaving the garage door open, I waited until all four bears were in the back of the building just starting towards my tent. Then I popped out of the open door right next to the tent and yelled at them - "Hey, get outa here! Go on, Git!"

I was all ready to scoot into the door and slam it if mama decided to make *me* git. Fortunately, off they went into the woods, never to come around again so far as I was aware. After that, I was even more careful to wash my dishes and clean up immediately after every meal. Also, I tried to avoid having overly smelly food around such as sausage, bacon, etc.

One of the other Fort Wilkins rangers of the early 1970's was not so lucky. Greg Tobin was staying in the Fort Wilkins bachelor's quarters in 1972, but he was always wishing to be staying out in the forest instead. Part way through the summer he moved out of the quarters and set up a camp in the woods east of Lake Fanny Hooe. He really wanted to be alone out in the woods to more fully experience nature.

Well, it's a good thing that Greg wasn't in his camp when one of the nature experiences occurred. He returned from work one evening to find his entire camp literally destroyed, lock, stock and barrel. While he was at work, what was undoubtedly a fairly large bear let Greg know what it thought about his encroaching into its territory. It did such a thorough job of destruction, that the only things Greg was able to salvage from his former camp were two well chewed Peterson's field guides (for birds and flowers as I recall), and the aluminum poles from his former tent.

Greg was really upset, not so much from the loss of almost all of his worldly goods, but because he could not live out in the woods where he preferred to be. I honestly don't know if the bear involved was just giving Greg a little hint to move elsewhere, or if Greg had been sloppy in his housekeeping, which invited a bear to chew up everything he owned. In any event, Greg's tent poles were still under the bachelor quarters porch when I left Fort Wilkins in the spring of 1974 to work at Porcupine Mountains State Park. They may still be there. (They were definitely gone as of April, 1992.)

STANDING SMALL

Imagine a small forty pound bear showing up all of a sudden in the day use area of Fort Wilkins State Park during the middle of a busy summer day. Not very likely, you say. But it did actually happen in 1972.

The bear wandered in from the surrounding forest and somehow got spooked into running further into the picnic area. It ended up in a tree about half way between the toilet building and the parking area. Naturally people gathered around to watch it, and it was very frightened. The rangers decided to try capturing it to remove it from the park.

One of the summer employees of the park, Jim Shea, decided that it was a small enough bear that he could climb the tree and grab the cub by the scruff of the neck. We never got to find out if such a feat were possible - that is, the actual grabbing of the bear. Long before Jim could get into a good position in the tree to grab at it, and after considerable effort, the bear had out maneuvered him, hissed and growled at him, taken a couple of swipes toward him with its claws, and urinated upon him from above. Jim's spirits were no longer up to the attempt, and he gave up.

Next, the rangers tried to trap the bear in one of the regular DNR bear live traps. This wasn't easy since the bear was still in the tree. A snow fence was placed around the tree, with the only exit into the trap. The trap was baited with favorite bear goodies - peanut butter and fruit. The only problem was that this particular trap had a defective release mechanism (seems like they all do), and it had to be released by pulling on a rope. The park, believe it or not, only had a 20 foot long piece of rope which was in very poor shape. This was strung out away from the trap and laid on the ground. One of the rangers, the author, laid on the ground and waited until the bear went into the trap. The only problem was that the bear would not come down with anyone that close to him - not after Jim had gone up after him.

Next we tried laying the rope towards the closest tree, behind which the ranger hid until the bear came down. The bear finally did come down but would not go into the trap while a ranger was watching him from behind the tree. So the ranger hid completely out of sight and relied on the other rangers to wave to him when the bear went into the trap. Eventually the bear went in, the rangers yelled, and the hidden ranger ran over and yanked on the rope, which broke. The bear had run out of the trap before the rope was reached anyway, so it was no great loss.

Our final try at getting the cub out of the tree and picnic area was successful. Realize that during all of the previous attempts there were quite a few people nearby watching our failures and taking pictures of all this. This contributed to our lack of success as it kept the bear very edgy. What we did finally was simply to make all the people leave the picnic area so the bear might come down by itself. This worked admirably. We didn't even notice when the bear took off.

TEENAGE MUTANT NINJA BEARS

Jim Shea, who was involved in the above incident with the cub at Fort Wilkins, had a somewhat similar incident occur to him in the early 1960's at Fort Wilkins State Park. The park had trapped a bear which turned out to be a sow with three previous years cubs. The cubs were all up in one tree. Al Billings, Mac Frimodig, and Jim decided to put a fish net under the tree to catch the cubs. Then, Jim would climb up and shake the cubs out of the tree into the net. Sounds pretty simple and straightforward. Therefore, something had to go wrong.

Jim climbed the tree as planned. The three cubs got panicky. They started down the tree in a big hurry and climbed right over Jim. Ouch!, those claws are sharp! Once the cubs were below Jim, they rushed back up the tree and over Jim again. Ouch!, Ouch! Then, the cubs in quite a frenzy quickly repeated this whole process again. Ooooo! Ouch! Damn! Jim got some scratches as well as his name in the newspaper.

The cubs were all eventually captured using the planned method and were relocated with the their mother.

PINT SIZED MARAUDERS

Little bears such as the one described in *Standing Small* can look really cute and lovable, but their looks can be quite deceiving. I doubt that Jim Shea would have succeeded in any kind of grabbing of that creature without major structural damage to his body. I can remember a couple of other small bears which were not as frightened by people as that one was. One was a regular visitor to the Presque Isle Campground at the west end of the Porcupine Mountains State Park. This was in 1970. Harvey Garrison was a seasonal ranger who lived in the campground there with his family. He had five children and lived in a tent approximately 8 by 12 feet with a screened section about 10 feet square. The little bear which bothered him was around 75 pounds in weight.

This bear went into Harvey's tent on several occasions, always entering and leaving through a new hole that it tore in the screened part of the tent. Really, this was Harvey's own fault because he always had food in his tent which was an unintentional invitation to the bear. It was impossible for him not to have something smelling of food around since he lived right there with his growing and hungry kids.

A few years later there was another similar sized bear in that campground. This one became quite bold. He would go right onto an occupied campsite and start grabbing any food which was laying around. On one occasion a camper ran up to ranger Jack Komsi yelling about a bear at his site. Jack went to investigate and found the small bear on top of a picnic table eating and swatting paper plates all over the place. Jack thought he would scare off this little devil, so he grabbed a dead tree branch and went over towards it. The bear came off the table, but did not run away. Jack went right up to it and poked the branch in its direction. The bear bit the branch off. Jack wisely reconsidered the situation and backed away. He advised the camper to wait until the bear left on its own and then to clean up the mess. This bear was not going to run away when food was involved.

Small bear can and do cause **BIG** problems. As an example, take the yearling cub which settled in as backpack inspector at Mirror Lake in 1981. This bear was too young to have any tact or finesse. It just walked right into camp as soon as the campers had unshouldered their loads, and it took their packs - no muss, no fuss.

Some backpackers said that they had noticed the little bear as they came into the vicinity of Mirror Lake, so they passed up the first camping spot they found and went further along the lake shore. They thought that the little bear had gone on its way elsewhere. They picked a camping spot on the northeast shore of the lake. No sooner did they stop and set down their packs, than out of the woods rushes the little menace and seizes their packs.

There was an attempt made to teach this bear some manners. Since it was so bold and was hitting every camp at Mirror Lake, it was decided by the powers that be that the little bear would be easy to locate for an etiquette lesson. Two rangers went out to the lake in hopes of having the bear try to seize their pack. The idea was to whip out a megaphone and/or other noise making gear and give the bear a good scare when it showed up. Perhaps they would even chase it away from the Mirror Lake area. The plans were pretty tentative because neither one knew how the bear would react to any of this.

The two rangers who went on this mission talked to a couple of different campers upon reaching Mirror Lake. The little menace had already shown up and grabbed their packs. One of the campers had just lost their pack a couple of minutes before the rangers arrived. The couple at that camp were so shook up by the bear that they were collecting materials for a fire to scare it away in case it returned. This was a trick they undoubtedly picked up from watching movies in which wild beasts would not come near a human holding a burning stick in his hand. Since the bear had already gotten their packs, and they would not have put their packs into the fire to keep them from the bear, a fire was a complete waste of time. Besides, fires were illegal. Fires will not stop bear from grabbing packs any more than staring at the bear will.

The rangers figured that the bear would be easy to locate. But the bear did something that neither of them expected. It really surprised them - it did not show up!

RISKY BUSINESS

The Lake of the Clouds scenic area was home to a sow bear with two cubs during the summer of 1981. These bears regularly visited the scenic area parking lot and nearby picnic sites tipping over the trash barrels and making a mess. Since there were usually people around the scenic area, these particular bears became quite accustomed to people being around. By midsummer, they were wandering right into the middle of the parking lot at midday with hundreds of people around. This naturally caused quite a stir among the tourists who would start gathering around to take pictures of the "tame" bears. The bears basically paid no attention whatever to the people or to being watched, except on those occasions when the people crowded the cubs too closely.

It was this author's duty one beautiful summer day to attempt some crowd control during the bears' normal 2:00 P.M. daily visitation to the Lake of the Clouds parking lot. This was really an experience. It was almost amazing to see how many of the people behaved when the bears appeared.

The trio of bears came down from somewhere towards the overlook to the east and out into the parking area right near the walkway to the overlook. One of the cubs came out of the woods near the trash barrel, which was just east of the walkway entrance. The sow did not leave the woods, but went behind some bushes right behind that trash can. The other cub was further to the east and reached its sibling at the can by walking along the sidewalk. (Note: the present rock walls next to the parking lot sidewalk did not exist back in 1981).

People came from all over the parking area and formed a semicircle around the two cubs, which were the only bears visible to them. The tourists started getting pretty excited. One young man came running from the west with his camera in his left hand and holding his girlfriend's (wife's?) hand in his right. Just as he got near the cubs, he sort of flung his gal forward toward the cubs as he raised his camera for a picture of them.

Mama bear didn't like this crowding around her cubs at all, and she popped up on her hind legs from behind the bushes quickly with a growl. Everyone backed off a little and surprisedly gasped, "Ooooh!" As soon as Mama saw that everything was okay, she went back to whatever it was she was doing. Meanwhile, the young man had grabbed his girlfriend's hand again while everyone was stepping back. He practically dragged her all the way around the outside of the crowd to the east side of the semicircle, where he flung her towards the cubs again from the opposite side for a picture. The lady didn't seem to be liking this at all.

I put the megaphone on and advised the people to get back a little further so as not to disturb the bears and to allow everyone to get a picture. Never having been assigned this type of crowd control duty before, I was not sure what kind of behavior to expect from the tourists. The above display on the part of the park visitors brought the problems involved into clear focus very quickly. The park visitors were assuming that these bears were actually tame. These types of problems became worse as the summer progressed - Julie Simmons, a summer ranger at the Porkies, reported that later in the season the tourists were actually petting these cubs in the parking lot.

While I was pondering the unexpected behavior of the park visitors which I had just witnessed, an older gentleman came up to me and started talking about the very subject I was contemplating. He said he had seen even more strange doings involving a bear. Once when he was in the Great Smoky Mountains National Park, he had stopped at an overlook area and discovered a large bear with its body most of the way inside of a trash barrel munching on garbage. There were two boys about 13 years old nearby watching the bear. He said I probably wouldn't believe what was going on there, but that it was true. The boys were throwing stones at the barrel. Every time a stone would hit and bong off the barrel, the bear would let out a muffled growl from within the barrel, but he would not come out. The gentleman said he told the kids that what they were doing was dangerous. The bear might come out of there and go after them. To this, one of the boys replied, "Aw, that's nothing - watch this!" Whereupon the kid went over to the barrel and kicked the bear right in the rump. The bear let out a big growl and moved the barrel from side to side but did not come out. The gentleman thereupon left quickly without further words with the boys.

After what I had seen this day at Lake of the Clouds, I would have believed almost any bear story the old gentleman had told me. I was going to tell him a true story he probably would not believe concerning the sow and two cubs which we were watching near the trash barrel in the Lake of the Clouds parking lot, but I did not have an opportunity right then (see *Life Is Just A Car Full Of Food,* below).

COPPER COUNTRY BEARS - 5
CHICAGO TOURISTS - 0

There have been quite a few regrettable incidents involving bears and various tourists' vehicles. Particularly aggravating were those involving convertibles. Convertibles are definitely not the best bet for motor transport in bear country. They are so easy to get into, do little to contain food smells, and they just don't hold up well at all to any bear pranks. Imagine a brand new rag top sportscar with the top all crushed in due to a fat bear sitting on it. Well, let me tell you, **that** is nothing compared to some of the things I have seen.

DANCING THE RAG

One time there was this brand new white Renault Le Car with black ragtop parked at the South Mirror Lake Trail parking area for about a week. You could see the paw prints going up the back and onto the top of the car. A bear had crushed the top in and then tore into the car where it further destroyed someone's dream machine. Apparently the owner had left something good smelling inside the vehicle for "safekeeping". Other bears got into the car also in search of food. Sometime between when the first bear and the last bear got onto and into the car, there had been a thunderstorm. The car was quite damp and was strewn with leaves and twigs.

Then there was the blue ragtop at Presque Isle Campground, into which a small bear entered right beside the back window. A loaf of bread had been left on the back seat, but the little bruin totally ignored it. Instead, he chewed up the entire interior of the car - the dashboard, the visors, the steering wheel, the seat backs, the doors - everything. What a mess it was. Perhaps bear are partial to the hide of the elusive nauga. Must have been pretty tasty vinyl. At least the critter left through the same hole he used to enter the vehicle, rather than making a matching pair.

LIFE IS JUST A CAR FULL OF FOOD

Hardtops and sedans have had their problems too. There was one intrepid backpacker who had rust holes in the bottom rear fenders of his auto, which was left at the Lake of the Clouds parking lot in 1981. The sow with two cubs easily located it by following the food smells emanating from the food cache stored in the trunk. It is not all that far, you know, from the outside of a rear fender to the inside of a car trunk. Not only could mama bear reach part of the cache herself, but the cubs could go right inside the car's trunk after mama peeled some of the fender metal up banana style. What fun and what a treat it must have been for the bears.

The owner of the car came back two weeks later with the same car, having done some Bondo repair work on the back fenders in the meantime. Once again he had a food cache in the trunk. The repair job did not hold up too well because the same thing happened all over again. I can just imagine the cubs thoughts when they saw the car again - "Look Mama, a banana."

A different bear also got into the act this trip. Prior to the sow and cubs getting to the car, this bear, which had a floppy ear (see *Something Wild* for how it got the floppy ear), took a liking to the vinyl top on the car. Then again, maybe it was just trying to get inside at the food. In any event, it helped to teach the rusty car owning backpacker a lesson which he would not ignore a second time. When the sow and cubs were not around (the sow would chase this bear away whenever she saw it), this bear climbed up on the vinyl roof and thoroughly clawed the roof all up. There is something about vinyl that brings out the destructive urge in bears. The sow also broke in a window and got inside the car. Well, as luck would have it, there happened to be a tourist who was watching while the sow and cubs vandalized the car. He even took pictures of the entire episode. Then he left a note for the car's owner telling him to write the photographer for the pictures in case he wanted to know what happened to his car.

Another sad case involved a new yellow compact car which had been parked by a backpacker at the Lake Superior Trailhead for almost two weeks. Someone broke into the car to steal a tape player and broke out the driver's side window in the process. In the back seat, the backpacker had left some food, the wonderful aroma of which attracted several bears into the vehicle. This was an especially disheartening mess. No wonder the ranger wrote the following in his notebook - "The bears are winning!"

BLAME IT ON RIO

One of the very worst bear/vehicle messes that this author is aware of was the result of an incident at the Copper Harbor dump. This occurred in the mid 1970's. A typical tourist went to the dump with a box of cookies for feeding the bears. He was driving a brand new custom van. When he got to the dump, he parked as close to a good sized bear as he could get, hopped out and tossed some cookies to the bear to attract it a little closer. The bear responded by coming a little closer, but not close enough to satisfy the tourist's desires to be near a bear. The tourist moved a little closer towards the bear still tossing it a cookie every now and then, and the bear came a little closer. Unfortunately, the tourist ran out of cookies without getting the bear to come as close as the tourist wanted.

The tourist turned around, stepped back to his van and hopped into the front seat. When he shut the drivers door, he heard a muffled noise back in the van. On looking around behind him he was nose to nose with a medium sized black bear which had climbed into his open van door while he was out feeding cookies to the other bear. Both the tourist and the bear panicked! The tourist jumped out and slammed the van door shut. The bear started clawing at the windows in an effort to get out of his fancy trap! It proceeded to claw, chew, urinate on, defecate in, as well as slosh saliva all over the entire interior of the custom van in its unsuccessful attempts to get out.

The damage being inflicted upon the van's interior was very evident to the tourist and other onlookers. They were all afraid to open a door for the bear's egress lest the bear might continue inflicting damage upon them when it got out. After many, many minutes of the bear frantically clawing up the inside of the van, another tourist who was watching all of this got up the courage to open one of the van's back doors and run. The bear came out immediately and ran away. The van's owner went to Fort Wilkins State Park just east of Copper Harbor the following day and demanded that the state pay for the damages to his van. Why blame the damage on Michigan? Why not blame it on Copper Harbor? Or on Keweenaw County? Or . . .

There is only one thing worse than a bear in a vehicle, and that is a bear in a building.

LIKE A BULL IN A CHINA SHOP

There are several "bear inside building" incidents that have come to the author's attention. Two occurred at Copper Harbor, Michigan. The first one was in the early 1970's. The details are sketchy, but there is no doubt that this occurred. A sow with two cubs entered the storage section of a restaurant and got into the flour. Supposedly they looked a lot like polar bears when they emerged. Of course, this was after they had made a tremendous mess.

The other incident occurred in mid September, 1985 at the Fort Wilkins State Park Concession. There are more details available on this event. The concession is a stone and wood building located between the parking lot and old Fort Wilkins. At the time of the incident, there were five couples all over 60 years old in the store. All of a sudden, out of nowhere, a small bear came crashing through the store's screen door and ran around inside trying to get out of the windows. The store's windows are metal sash type with small panes of glass. Thus the bear was unable to get out of the store through the windows, and it refused to leave through the door the way it entered.

Very shortly after the bear raced into the store and started knocking down merchandise and climbing the walls, the store manager and the older couples inside quickly exited the premises. Meanwhile, the bear tore up the place in its efforts to get out of the windows. It knocked down pottery and other souvenir items, clawed up the woodwork, and ripped a light fixture out of the ceiling.

The people who fled the store and quite a few others from elsewhere in the park congregated outside the building trying to get pictures of the bear inside as it ransacked the place. The bear finally got into a back storage room, which it was impossible to scare it out of. Bob Hill, the park assistant manager, had to destroy the animal by shooting it through a storeroom window. The bear was a 100 pound male. It had done approximately three hundred dollars worth of damage to the store and its contents.

The bear was most likely being chased by dogs prior to entering the store. It had run through the east campground, the picnic area, and the parking lot. As it ran down the walkway towards the concession, it encountered an elderly couple who were just past the store's entrance. When it saw them, it turned abruptly and crashed through the store's screen door. One of the older ladies who first saw the bear initially thought it was a cute pet of some kind. She quickly changed her opinion upon seeing its very unpetlike behavior.

OUTRAGEOUS FORTUNE

In early summer 1985, a scraggly two and a half year old bear of about 85 pounds started regularly showing up in the evenings at the Presque Isle trash bin. All of the rangers had seen him about during the day at one time or another. But every evening he showed up right around dusk to dig into the garbage. While he was a big hit with the campers, who gathered on foot with flashlights and in their cars to watch him, he was a problem for the park staff. This was due to the fact that he had to tear the top of the garbage bin off to get at the goodies inside. Also, he was very sloppy. His normal method was to grab a bag of garbage and drag it out and back into the woods behind the bin where he would tear everything apart. This left a trail of trash from the bin out into the woods. The idea of the trash bin is to provide for easy pickup of the trash. The park staff do not like having to scour the nearby woods picking up the garbage off the ground.

Ranger Mark Hedstrom dubbed the little rascal Boo Boo, and the name stuck. It wasn't too long before Boo Boo decided to try some of the garbage prior to the campers throwing it into the bin. At the Presque Isle Campground, virgin timber forest comes right up behind the camp sites, which were cut right out of a virgin timber area in Porcupine Mountains Wilderness State Park. Boo Boo could sneak right up to the sites and grab garbage bags that were carelessly left lying about. During these types of little raids, he discovered that the campers also had food which they sometimes carelessly left lying about. He liked camper food even better than garbage.

As mentioned before, these bear problems always go from bad to worse. Boo Boo grew very fast due to his nourishing and plentiful food supply. When he first came, the garbage bin was a goodly supply for him. However, the garbage amounts actually increased because he was there. This was due to the word spreading that a bear regularly showed up every evening. Many campers came just to see him. But as he grew bigger, his appetite increased. He learned that he could get food from the campers by visiting them at supper time and snitching it if they didn't put it into a vehicle. So he started paying regular visits to the campground during the day as well as visiting the trash bin in the evening.

He was becoming a first rate pest, but the campers loved every minute of it. It got so bad that Boo Boo practically lived in the campground. He was there somewhere or other during a good portion of the day. The author happened to be working an afternoon shift that year. He could almost always tell exactly where Boo Boo was when he drove into the campground by one of two methods. If there was a large crowd of campers gathered somewhere in the campground, that was one sure sign. They would all be gathered to take pictures of Boo Boo. The other method was not quite as simple, but equally foolproof. It involved looking at the campers who were cooking meals. If they were all keeping an eye out towards a particular direction, Boo Boo was bound to be over that way. They were keeping prepared to put the food away at a moment's notice if Boo Boo came their way. These two methods for locating the bear relate to the latter part of the summer after Boo Boo decided that Presque Isle Campground was a great place to live. Eventually he was hanging around the campground all day long, continually trying to snitch food and coolers from the campers.

Boo Boo would make regular rounds of the campground. At first, he would sneak out from the woods onto the sites, going from site to site all the way around the campground. It was an ongoing challenge for the campers to be able to eat in peace. Boo Boo had the trash bin at night, as well as the picnic area trash cans and the campers to pick on all day. Later, after losing a lot of his fear of the people, he wandered all over the place. Now don't assume that attempts were not made to control Boo Boo. He was trapped on four different occasions and released elsewhere. But he always returned, usually within a day. Part of the reason for this was that he loved the place so much because of the food and part because he was always released within the park. The rangers repaired the trash bin the first two times he was trapped, but they gave up after that knowing full well he would be back.

Boo Boo was becoming a pretty big fellow. At first he had to tear apart the bin doors to get at the garbage. Now that he was growing up, he could sort of crush the doors in. The more of a pest he became, the more word spread about the certainty of seeing a bear at Presque Isle, and the more people came. The more people, the more food, and the fatter Boo Boo got. The fat bear get fatter. He started getting into trouble too. On one occasion, he was annoying some campers as the author happened to drive by in a park pickup truck. There was an attempt to scare him by driving up to him and blowing the horn. This resulted in his turning around, walking to a tree behind him, and then turning back to look at the truck. He wasn't exactly quivering with fright. Actually, I think he was getting quite used to people doing such things to try to frighten him away. It wasn't working any more.

On one occasion he really scared some people. A camper had gone fishing in the Presque Isle River early in the morning, leaving his family asleep at the campsite. His wife was in a tent trailer, and two children were in a tent. He had unwisely left a cooler on the picnic table which was between the tent and camper. When he returned to his site, there was Boo Boo tearing apart his cooler. The table with the cooler on it was right next to the tent with the kids in it. The camper panicked and immediately went around to get the kids out of the tent. Boo Boo apparently interpreted this as an attempt to get the food away from him, because he would not even let the guy approach the tent. The camper got more upset, but he could not get near the tent without subjecting himself to the wrath of Boo Boo.

The camper yelled to wake up his children and told them to stay in the tent because a bear was outside. As soon as Boo Boo finished off the campers food, he went on to better pickings, and the camper got his kids out of the tent. I bet he never lets them sleep in a tent again! This gentleman was really angry after this incident, and let the park staff know it.

Since Boo Boo had already returned to Presque Isle after having been trapped four times, he was not going into the trap any more. So a different type of attempt was made to get Boo Boo to leave the area. The tranquilizer gun was put into use. It turns out that there were at least three attempts to tranquilize Boo Boo.

The first attempt apparently occurred the very afternoon the tranquilizer gun was available. Ranger Jim Richardson and Park employees Bob and Dave went to Presque Isle for the initial attempt to get the bear. Boo Boo was right beside a tree when they arrived. Dave offered to do the shooting because he had been in the army. He fired, and Boo Boo moved away from the tree and sat down upon an old tree stump or little hillock further into the woods. Jim and Bob followed Boo Boo and stopped about thirty feet away from him. Boo

Boo sat patiently watching the three men, his head tilting a little from side to side as if wondering what they were up to. Jim and Bob figured it would just be a few moments before Boo Boo keeled over under the influence of the tranquilizer. They were sure he was getting lightheaded by the way he was tilting his head. As soon as Boo Boo went to sleep, they could put a rope around him and drag him back and into the bear trap.

After a short time of bear and men watching each other, Dave, who had shot Boo Boo, finished putting away the tranquilizer gun and came towards where Jim and Bob were standing. On the way he passed directly next to the tree which Boo Boo had been standing near when shot at. There, in the tree trunk, the dart intended for Boo Boo was stuck. Dave had missed (it should be noted that he had been a photographer in the army.) Dave informed Jim and Bob that Boo Boo had not been shot with the tranquilizer gun. Realizing that Boo Boo was not getting drowsy, Jim and Bob backed away from the bear. Since it was late in their working day, the men decided to try again another day.

The second attempt is a little sketchy on the details, but one of the seasonal employees named Gary Cvengross was involved. Gary decided to do a little target practice all by himself with the tranquilizing gun using Boo Boo as the target. He shot Boo Boo once and waited a few minutes while Boo Boo ate garbage out in the woods. Boo Boo was still eating, so Gary shot Boo Boo again. After the second dose of tranquilizer, Boo Boo started showing signs of disorientation. Gary prepared to go get Boo Boo.

First, he opened his car door. There were onlookers from the Presque Isle Campground as this was going on. One of them asked him why he was opening his car door. "You never can tell what will happen," he replied. "Boo Boo might wake up, so I might have to run over, hop into the car and shut the door right away." The onlookers backed further away. Then Gary went into the woods following the obviously groggy Boo Boo and tied his only piece of rope around Boo Boo. He tugged the hefty bruin out of the woods towards the waiting bear live trap. He found out right away that it was no simple task to pull a 150 pound bear through the woods.

As he tugged the bear closer to the trap, he had problems getting Boo Boo up into the opening. None of this was going as smoothly or as quickly as Gary had envisioned it. Boo Boo revived slightly, just enough to recognize the trap. The bruin awkwardly crawled away towards the woods. Cvengross was fit to be tied. He took off to prepare another dose of the tranquilizer.

On his return, Cvengross immediately shot Boo Boo again. Then he tilted the live trap door downwards so as to have an easier time of dragging Boo Boo into it. Gary rechecked his car door, went to the edge of the woods where Boo Boo had crawled and was now dozing, and re-secured the rope around the bruin. Gary was a rather muscular young man and managed to get Boo Boo over to the trap, string the rope through it and pull Boo Boo all the way inside. Unfortunately, the trap was now tilted too much. The rope broke, and Boo Boo slid out the trap's door. Once again Boo Boo became restless. He slowly crawled back towards the woods in his drug induced daze. This ended the second attempt to tranquilize him.

By now it was getting late in the summer season. Around the middle of August in a third attempt to tranquilize Boo Boo, Rangers Pete Kemppainen, Jerry Bukoski, Jim Richardson, and Auto Mechanic Jim Rogan went down to the garbage bin armed with the tranquilizer gun and prepared to get Boo Boo out of Presque Isle. The plan was the same as before; tranquilize him, tie a rope around him, and drag him into the trap. Then he would be hauled far away, hopefully never to return.

By now Boo Boo was getting a little gun shy, so it took him awhile to come out into the open. When the rangers approached Boo Boo with the tranquilizer gun, he decided to climb a tree. This was not his normal behavior, which was simply to stand and watch, but since he had been shot at several times before, and drugged once, Boo Boo decided to get into a more "safe" location.

Jerry Bukoski got a good shot at Boo Boo in a low branch of a tree. The end of the tranquilizer gun was no more than six feet away from the bear. He couldn't miss. After he was shot, Boo Boo came down from the tree branch and wandered back into the woods about 50 yards and stood watching his pursuers. Jerry, and the two Jims followed after the bear with the rope and kept alert for signs of his weakening. Boo Boo sat down, and the rangers and mechanic started closing in a little.

Pete, who had stayed back near where Boo Boo was shot at, noticed something on the ground under the tree. It was the dart, and it was completely full of the tranquilizing drug. Apparently it had bounced off Boo Boo, and so Boo Boo was not drugged. Pete yelled, "Yoo hoo! Fellas, look at this," while holding up the dart. When Pete told them what he was holding, Jerry, Jim and Jim quickly backed off from their close approach to rope Boo Boo. Thus, the third and final (as far as I know) tranquilization attempt of Boo Boo came to a halt.

Clearly, there is a certain art to tranquilizing bears, and it is quite evident that no one who attempted it at the Porkies back in 1985 was an artist. After this attempt, Boo Boo started making himself more scarce around Presque Isle. He didn't like being the target, apparently. The number of campers was starting to drop off as it normally does at this time of year anyway, so his pickings were getting a little slimmer.

An attempt was also made to simply scare Boo Boo away from the Presque Isle area. This involved bringing in dogs which would hopefully chase Boo Boo somewhere else - anywhere else. This undertaking got fouled up in its very earliest stages due to the large number of skunks which hang around the Presque Isle Campground. In all of their attempts to get rid of Boo Boo, the rangers got skunked - sometimes figuratively, sometimes literally.

Well, Boo Boo got very big by the end of this summer. The last time the author saw him (probably during the first week of September), he didn't realize it was even the same bear. He was around 200 pounds, had a shiny black coat, and was so chubby you could see the fat rippling under his coat as he walked.

Boo Boo did not return to Presque Isle the following summer, thank goodness. If the bear had, it probably would have been a dangerous summer for the campers. The author believes Boo Boo was taken by hunters the opening day of early bear season - September 10th. One of the bear hunters camping at the park told him about the strange behaving bear their party had shot on opening day. They were putting out some bait when they spotted a bear. The bear didn't run away. It came right towards them and their smelly bait. They could hardly believe their eyes. It was a bear which exactly fit Boo Boo's description, both physical and behavioral. It went right after the bait and completely ignored the hunters. They even went and got a video camera to film the bear prior to shooting it since it obviously was not going to run off.

It is probably a good thing that hunters got Boo Boo because the park would undoubtedly have had to destroy him the next summer. Boo Boo may not have been a boar. Instead, "she" may have been a sow which would have come back with cubs the next year. In that case, she would probably have been another terrible problem bear much like the one involved in a Mike Patterson's death in 1978 (see *She Was The Terror Of The Porkies*). No one needs problems like that.

ALL THE WRONG MOVES

The first serious bear related injury incident at Porcupine Mountains State Park occurred in 1975. It involved Paul Cameron, a sixteen year old lad, who was backpacking alone. Note that both of the really serious bear incidents which have occurred in the Park involved young male backpackers who were on lone camping trips. Backpacking alone is *not* recommended. But that was only his first mistake. Paul had a habit of cooking and eating in his tent. He had even spilled cooking oil in it previously. Apparently he was unaware of possible problems with food loving bears.

Paul hiked to the Mirror Lake area. He set up his tent about 200 yards west of the Mirror Lake four bunk cabin. It started to rain, so he hopped into his tent to cook supper. This was back in the heyday of the big Mirror Lake boar, Bruno. As you can imagine, Paul was a sitting duck for that bear.

Exactly what occurred at Mirror Lake between Paul and the big bear is unknown, except that Bruno got some of Paul's food. Based upon his later actions, this probably occurred in the late afternoon after Paul's supper. Paul was not the type of camper to worry about hanging up his food, nor is it likely that he took great care in cleaning up after his meal. The big bear undoubtedly had easy pickings and scared the daylights out of Paul. So much so in fact that Paul packed up all his gear after losing his food and left the Mirror Lake area.

He probably hiked out of the interior on the Government Peak Trail, because he ended up at that trail head on M-107. He set up his tent there, not too far away from the trailhead trash barrel. It is quite possible that it was dark when Paul set up his tent there, but this is not known for sure.

In the morning, Paul woke up to noises outside his tent. It was light out. The noises, he decided, were those of a bear prowling around. Sniffing noises, scratching noises, little huffs, and assorted other bear noises. Fortunately, Paul thought, this bear would not be able to get the rest of his food because he had brought all his gear into his tent with him this time, including his food. That was a terrible mistake.

The noises got closer, and Paul decided to play dead. Somewhere he had heard to play dead if a bear attacks you. This bear had not attacked him, but he was going to play dead right off the bat.

The bear finally got right up next to his tent. The tent contained Paul, his pack, and what was left of his food supply. The bear was a smallish female with two cubs. She weighed about 120 pounds and did what most bear would have done - find the food. The smell was coming from the tent, so she started chewing and tearing on the tent. Meanwhile Paul was inside playing dead. What with the spilled oil smell, the previous evening's noodles and beef supper smell, and the smell from the rest of his food, perhaps the sow could not determine that there was a human in the tent.

Paul kept playing dead while the sow chewed its way right around his tent, and while it started to chew on him right through the tent walls. He thought he was doing the right thing playing dead. Now he knew he was in big trouble. The bear kept chewing through the tent, sometimes on him and sometimes on his gear. He rolled himself outside when he got a chance, but the bear came over and chewed on his arms and chest. Now he decided that playing dead was going to lead to the real thing. He kicked and screamed, got up and ran.

The bear came after him. He ran across the pavement nearby and climbed up into an aspen. The bear followed him. In desperation he jumped to a nearby tree. The bear went back down the first tree and came over to the new tree he was in. It started up that tree, but then went back down and returned across M-107 to his tent. There it proceeded to tear apart all his gear.

Paul had received many bite wounds on his arms, chest and shoulders. He stayed in the tree until he managed to flag down a passing tourist's car. They took him to the Park Headquarters, and then he was taken to the hospital. The nearest Conservation Officer was contacted. He and Park Ranger Dave Peloso went to the trailhead where they found the bear still tearing up Paul's gear. The sow was destroyed, and plans were discussed on how to capture the cubs. Sadly, they both died while being tranquilized and falling from the tree.

Hindsight is always 20/20 of course, but Paul probably could not have made more errors which cause problems with bears. If he had not had any food smells coming from his tent, the incident would undoubtedly not have occurred. But why, you may ask, did the bear go after him when he decided to quit acting like a meat loaf?

Look at it from the bear's point of view, if that is possible. You have two kids to feed, and you yourself are hungry continually. You come upon some great smelling food. You are not familiar with this type of food, so you start trying to locate it exactly. The smell is all over this tent which you proceed to chew upon. As you start getting to the good part, there is yelling and a man is right in your food supply. He is a threat to you, your food, and to your kids. You chase him away.

Then again maybe she was going to eat Paul. But it was only because he smelled like a pot roast and acted like one too. In all likelihood, if Paul had made some noise when he knew there was a bear around, the bear would have left. But even if she had not left, he should have gotten up and let the bear know he was there. It would not have been the first time a camper wisely left to let a bear tear up his gear for the food in it.

Why didn't playing dead work? Playing dead is a possible method of saving one's life in situations where a large bear, generally a grizzly, is attacking a person with full intentions of eating them. Grizzly often kill large animals, then stash the corpse under some brush or dirt, and return later to eat. Black bears have also been known to exhibit this behavior. If one were to play dead in such a situation, one might not be killed, and one might be able to escape later. But that was not the situation in Paul's case.

The bear involved was a 120 pound black bear sow with two small cubs. There are no grizzlies in the Porkies, thank God. The sow was attracted by the food smell, and she was undoubtedly not attacking a man with full intentions of eating him. Her behavior around the tent was consistent with other black bear actions relating to getting food. Her later behavior in chasing Paul up a tree is also consistent with black bear behavior relating to protection of food supply and of cubs. Paul, by playing dead, unknowingly lured the sow into his close proximity because of the food smells permeating his equipment and clothes. This resulted in his personal injury.

Personal injury is a possibility whenever bears get too close to people, and that is the main reason for the rules regarding never feeding bears and taking precautions with food supplies. The next time you are tempted to toss goodies to a bear or leave your food on the ground, remember - the person who gets hurt by that bear may be you. Also remember that you are helping the bear become fearless which will result in its being prematurely killed.

ON THE BRINK OF DISASTER

Dave Peloso is an experienced trapper who has encountered numerous bears in the woods through the years. He is used to seeing bears and watching them take off and run away when they realize a human is near. In April of 1987, he saw one which did not take off and run away.

He was checking his trap line and had his dog Sally, a Chesapeake Bay retriever, with him. Having just removed two beaver carcasses from traps, he was going to leave them to dry as he checked other traps and set some new ones. His dog was about 150 feet away from him and started barking at something. There were no leaves out yet, so he could see pretty clearly off through the woods. He could see his dog, but not what it was barking at. The dog was standing on top of a slight mound and continued barking although it did not seem really upset. Dave was just getting ready to leave the spot where the two carcasses were when he took a few steps towards his dog to see what it was barking at.

Then he found out. A fairly large bear which had been hidden by the mound his dog was on stood up in the distance. The dog barked a little more zestily now, and the bear turned and started to climb a good sized Aspen tree. It only went up a short distance though. Dave called his dog which came running back towards him. Meanwhile, the bear came down from the tree and took a few steps towards Dave and his dog instead of running away. Dave yelled and banged his axe against a tree trunk, and the dog turned around about halfway back from the bear and started barking again. After lots of axe banging, yelling and barking, the bear very slowly started walking away from them.

Dave noticed that the behavior of this bear was very different from that of the many others which he had seen in the woods. He considered the time of year - bears were out of hibernation and were hungry in the spring. He considered that the bear could smell the beaver carcasses which were behind him, and it undoubtedly wanted them. Also, he noticed that the bear had not apparently noticed his scent, which was due to the fact that he tried to hide his scent using potent natural (skunk) scents.

He thought the bear had behaved rather strangely, but he still set out to finish what he planned to do earlier. He took his carcasses with him instead of leaving them to dry since the bear was about. At his next stop he saw good beaver sign and set about putting in a trap. He was standing out in the water when his dog which was a few feet away on the shore started to bark. He looked up, and there beyond the dog off in the woods was the same bear coming towards them.

This really shook Dave up. This bear was not afraid of him at all, and it wanted to eat the beaver carcasses - possibly Dave too, since he smelled so much like one. The bear was somewhat apprehensive of the dog but not very much so of Dave.

Dropping the trap set, Dave grabbed the beaver carcasses, put one in his pack, flopped the other over his shoulder, and got out of there fast. He later decided to pull all of his traps for this season since the quality of the fur was beginning to deteriorate any way. Also, he decided to carry a firearm with him whenever he went out trapping again.

RAIDERS OF THE LOST CAMP

This author had a very interesting experience on the Government Peak Trail in Porcupine Mountains Wilderness State Park back in the summer of 1975. I was on my way out to survey the condition of the foot trail, trail signs, bridges, etc. Having hiked about two miles from the trailhead on an exceptionally nice day, I was just getting up into the higher areas along the upper Carp River when a group of three young men who were day hiking came into view.

Being in uniform, the hikers came up to me and started complaining right away about how sloppy some of the backpackers were. They had found a camping spot about a half mile further south near the Government Peak Trail where the campers had really littered and partied. The young men said that the campers had thrown all of their trash around the campsite, even some of their clothes. There were also cans all over the campsite which had been shot up with a .22 caliber firearm according to them. Then the hikers displayed a pack frame which they had retrieved from the campsite. The campers had even left that behind.

Since this disaster area of a campsite was just a little off the main trail, clear directions were obtained from the day hikers on how to locate it. Then I proceeded on my way southward. It seemed rather odd to me that campers would have left their pack behind. Then again, not very many packers behave the way these must have done in order to make the mess described by the hikers. I was very careful to keep an eye out for the tiny side trail which led to the camp spot they had discovered, and I found it without any trouble.

Sure enough, the campers had left a tremendous mess. A catsup bottle broken on a rock was the first thing I noticed. There were clothes and trash strewn all over the camp site. The pack sack from the frame which the hikers had retrieved was all torn up, and there were cans strewn helter skelter around the campsite just as described by the hikers. However, they had not been shot up with a firearm as the hikers had presumed. There were no spent cartridge cases anywhere at the site.

This was not a camp at which backpackers had partied and made a mess at. Instead, it was a camp which a bear had destroyed. All of the mess and destruction had been the result of a bear incident. The "bullet" holes in the cans were tooth marks from having been chewed up by a bear! Except for the campers, their tent, their sleeping gear, and the pack frame removed by the day hikers, everything the campers brought to this site was still here. As is usual with me, my mind immediately went to work trying to hypothesize what possibly could have happened here.

My guess is that a bear came into camp while the packers were either setting up their tent or while they were in their tent, and it proceeded to destroy all of the camping gear and food which they had so carelessly left lying around the site. The campers were probably frightened out of their wits. They undoubtedly took off with whatever clothes they had on, grabbed the tent and sleeping bags, and left everything else behind for the bear to do with as he pleased. The bear tore up the pack sack and the clothes, chewed open the cans, and swatted bottles around. The only thing left undamaged was a bottle of cooking oil. There was no evidence that any precautions had been taken to keep the smell of the food out of the clothing. The food supplies carried by these campers reinforced the conclusion that they were not overly familiar with backpacking or camping in bear territory. A glass bottle of ketchup? All food in tin cans? Seems like a pretty heavy load to carry so far to me.

I could see why the hikers thought that the cans had been shot up with a .22 caliber firearm. There were numerous holes approximately bullet size all over the cans; they were literally chewed up and torn apart. There was one can which was not chewed open. It was a large pressurized can of "6-12 Insect Repellent" which had one set of bite mark holes in it. Evidently the bear did not like the taste of insect repellent which undoubtedly was a relatively unpleasant surprise.

Well, I tidied up the place as best I could. Rangers usually carry trash bags for just such uses, but I did not have enough with me for this mess. While the campers had not made the mess, it is pretty clear that they had been very sloppy with their gear, especially their food. They had left it right next to their tent area, and had not made any visible efforts to keep it away from animals.

I stacked the packaged trash for a future trip in to pick it up, and proceeded on the Government Peak Trail. After seeing that mess, I couldn't get my mind off wondering how big the bear might have been, had it done this during the night, did it hang around this area, and was it nearby right now? I was getting a little edgy about bears being around. Memories surfaced of the hike on the Lost Lake Trail about a week earlier when I had seen very large, very fresh bear tracks going the same direction I was going. That time I had wondered why I was continuing on when most certainly there was a large bear somewhere up ahead. All these thoughts prompted me to keep an eye out for convenient sized trees that I might be able to climb in an emergency. I still had to walk eight and a half miles. Needless to say, I was quite alert for the rest of my hike, which was otherwise uneventful.

THE CURSE OF THE BLACK BEAR

BEAR WARS

Not every bear could claim all of the achievements of the one I am about to discuss. This particular bear started out begging for food by the Carp Lake Mine picnic site along highway M-107 in Porcupine Mountains Wilderness State Park. It developed a set pattern of begging behavior which it utilized at other locations later on in 1978. Naturally, things progressed from bad to worse, that is, from begging to taking, while it was still at that location.

Dan Castle of Ontonagon was a crew leader at Porcupine Mountains Wilderness State Park in 1978. He was driving a park pickup truck down from Lake of the Clouds scenic area to the Union Bay service area when an unusually large collection of vehicles and people at the M-107 Mine Site picnic area caught his eye. On stopping, Dan saw a bear of about 200 pounds on top of a picnic table with its muzzle stuck into a picnic basket. The picnickers and others were all standing around watching and taking pictures.

As soon as Dan arrived in the park truck, everyone started asking him what he was going to do about the bear. They thought he was a ranger, and they expected him to "do something." Dan sort of felt obliged to do something, but he didn't quite know exactly what it was he should do. On checking in the back of the pickup truck he found a round pointed shovel and a steel grass whip. He took these out of the truck and prepared to chase the bear away with them. The people all got ready to watch and take pictures. One fellow even had a movie camera to record all the action.

Dan raised his tools up in the air, started banging them together, and ran at the bear, which was still on the picnic table tearing up someone's picnic supplies. The bear looked at him, very reluctantly got off the table, turned and leisurely moved about five feet into the low brush which surrounds that particular picnic site. Everyone thought Dan knew what he was doing, but Dan knew that he really did not know what he was doing. He was quite relieved that the bear was heading away from him. Dan followed the bruin up to the edge of the brush. The bear did not enter the brushy area too far. It stopped, turned, and stood up to face Dan. Whoa! It was taller than he was!

Dan was certain that the people could see his heart beating right through his shirt during this entire episode. He stood his ground hitting his grass whip and shovel together and told the picnickers to get their stuff out of there. They quickly complied, but were worried about their franks on the grill which were not yet done. Dan told them to forget about the franks. Then, the picnickers, the onlookers, and the guy who was filming all of this went their separate ways while Dan went down to tell the boss about the bear problem.

THE RANGERS STRIKE BACK

It was obvious by now that this bear was getting so close to people that it had to be trapped. That very day the Rangers set a live trap for him. Trapping a bear is usually very easy the first time and generally more difficult each succeeding time. Some bears learn a lot faster than others, and some seem never to learn at all. Thus some only get trapped once and never again. Others, like Boo Boo, can be trapped several times before they realize that they don't want to be hauled away from places where they are having so much fun. This particular bear was trapped easily the first time, but he was *never* trapped again. He was a very quick learner.

There was some kind of communications mixup when the park employees were informed where to release this bruin. Generally, bears are transported a long distance from where they are trapped before they are released. Otherwise, they will return right away and cause the same problems all over again. The idea is to get them away from the easy garbage pickings, campers' food, or handouts of food along the road, so they will return to mother nature's food sources. Instead of being released near the southeast end of the White River Road which is well away from the park, he was released on the northwest end of the road right in the middle of Porcupine Mountains Wilderness State Park. The Porkies had another major bear problem develop as a result of this mix-up.

THE RETURN OF THE BEAR

This bear was a large one at close to 200 pounds, and it had a distinctive white marking like an arrowhead on its chest (similar to the bear on the cover of this book). He was sometimes referred to as Whitepatch. Many black bears have such markings, but they are not always readily noticeable as on this one. As soon as he was released, he reverted to food begging and became a problem along the South Boundary Road. It was sort of like Yellowstone National Park out there for awhile. A tourist would come around the corner, and there would be this large bear sitting right in the middle of the road. Unlike other bears which would run away so you could not get a picture of them, this bear sat right in the middle of the road while the tourists got all excited, got out their cameras, and threw various morsels to him while they took pictures. It was a regular circus with lines of cars developing now and then.

Ranger Don Harris told me about one of the traffic jams he had observed which was caused by this bear. He had come around a corner in the virgin white pine area (between White Pine and Lost Creek outpost camps) along South Boundary Road. There was a line of vehicles up ahead, as well as people out all over the roadway. He stopped and went up to see what was going on. He found out right away. There, on the hood of the first car, the bear was sitting. Not too far from the bear was a little girl tossing it donuts. Everyone else was standing around taking pictures. Don told the people with the little girl to stop feeding the bear and leave because the bear was not tame. It would not want to quit eating just because the people ran out of donuts to give it. Then Don left.

While it sounds amazing that people would do something like this, it does happen. They just do not seem to realize the possible danger they are placing themselves in. Many years ago, at the same location this bear was trapped at, some man tried to place his child on a bear's back for a picture! That time the child was injured slightly, and the bear was destroyed.

Over the next few days, the white chested bear stayed close to the road and slowly traveled to the east. It was not long before he reached the White Pine Extension Outpost Campground. Here was a new treat - garbage - and people camping, and of course food! What a little paradise for him. He immediately made himself at home and as quickly became a super pest. No one could cook out there without losing their food. No one could camp out there without sharing their site with this 200 pound freeloader. Where does a 200 pound bear sleep? Anywhere he wants to!

Well, he didn't try to sleep in anyone's tent, but you can imagine the situation. He was so used to people tossing food to him that when anyone would throw a stone at him to scare him away, he would run up to it excitedly and sniff it expecting it to be food. Things got so bad, and the park received so many complaints, that we had to close down the campground because efforts to trap him failed. Whitepatch was not going back into our live trap.

As the campers disappeared and the food supply dried up, the bear meandered further east along the road to the next outpost campground - Lost Creek. The same situation developed all over again, with the same result - another campground closed. During his stay at the outposts, he had several opportunities to scare the hell out of various tourists - though not intentionally I am sure.

One time, a young couple set up camp at White Pine Outpost and then left to see the sights. When they returned to their camp later, it was demolished. The bear was sitting on their site devouring the last of their food from their cooler which they had left in their tent. The man got out of his VW Beetle and yelled at the bear which then came running toward him. The man jumped back into his yellow Beetle, and the bear ran up to it and climbed on top. While the lady went bananas, the guy started the car and put it in L for leap. He took off with a jerk, causing the bear to slide off the back. According to Don Harris, there were prominent claw marks from the roof all the way down the back of the car to prove it. Don talked to the couple at the Presque Isle Waterfalls area as they were leaving the park just after the incident. The lady was still hysterical.

Whitepatch had apparently expected some food from them. It was used to having food come flying out of car windows while it waited along the roadside. Not having any food fly out of the car towards him, just a man and a yell, the bruin apparently decided to go take the food out of the car. To this bear, cars meant food. Apparently he was starting to get impatient with cars that didn't mean food.

He was getting so impatient for food from vehicles along the road that he was almost "biting the hand that feeds him." He would no longer wait for tossed food. When the tossing ended, he eagerly reached into the vehicles for more. This ended the traffic jams, since no one wanted to contribute their nose to a bear just for a picture. After quite a few incidents, and after the campgrounds were closed for a week or so, the bear went elsewhere again due to lack of food. Once he left the roadsides, however, things really started to happen. The old boy wandered north into the park's interior where he ended up on the Government Peak Trail. It was there that he got himself into a real jam.

The author manned the Union Bay Campground Office back then. For two days in a row there was an unregistered bus in the campground in the morning. It was from one of those groups which takes inner city juvenile delinquents and makes self reliant wilderness types out of them. The bus was not supposed to be in the campground, but ended up there because one of the inner city youths ran away from his group on the interior. The driver took the youth to Union Bay Campground for the night. It turned out that the particular delinquent who was running away from his backpacking group did so because of a schizoid bear with a noticeable white patch on its chest which started hanging around their camp on the Government Peak Trail. There were around twenty persons in this group, or nineteen, depending on when you counted. The delinquent who split decided he would rather be somewhere else once the bear showed up. He undoubtedly had a lot of common sense.

THERE'S FOOD IN THEM THAR HILLS!

Whitepatch did not associate packs with food at first, but he did associate people with food. So when he saw the large camp of the inner city kids way out there in the woods, he was undoubtedly very happy because people had food and he was hungry. He knew they had food somewhere. He came into their camp, and it wasn't long at all before he learned that they were all carrying food in their packs. After that, the campers couldn't do anything. They could not cook or eat. They couldn't even get their packs or other gear, actually. It was obvious they could not stay in the interior, so they left their camping area and headed out, minus their equipment. The only equipment they had left with them was a fanny pack belonging to one of the leaders. Whitepatch was not so intent on consuming their food and destroying their equipment in the process that he was going to let them get away with something which might contain food. As I said, he was a fast learner. The bear went right after the leader who was forced to throw the pack to the bear to save himself from who knows what fate.

This bear encounter took place over a day and a half. Remember, one of the kids had run away at the first sight of Whitepatch and had been returned to the group the following day. Sometime during the encounter, the entire group of backpackers took off running down a hillside from the bear for some reason. Whitepatch ran right after them. As misfortune would have it, one of the youths, a young man with a leather jacket, slipped and fell down. The bear was on top of him instantly! Whitepatch was apparently excited by all the yelling and running. He held the man down with one paw while he sniffed him several times under each arm and beside the head. Since the youth had no food, Whitepatch left the young man and took off running after the rest of the group on down the hill. The young man was not physically harmed at all; psychologically though, who knows? With a rehabilitation program like this, there's little doubt this particular delinquent probably straightened right up after surviving the Porkies.

The group somehow managed to get back together and out of the interior. That is how their bus ended up in the Union Bay Campground for a second night in a row. The leaders of the group reported their situation to rangers, and the authorities decided that Whitepatch had crossed into the fearless zone. They sent out a bear patrol.

The bear patrol consisted of Jim Richardson, Dave Peloso, and Howard Meadowcroft, who were well armed. One of the group leaders accompanied them to the abandoned camping area, where they discovered a sea of trash and damaged equipment from the bear. The bear was nowhere around so they started back to the Union Bay area. When they reached the spot where the leader had thrown his fanny pack to the bear, the leader requested to stop and look around for it with an armed ranger to accompany him. The patrol members assured him not to worry, that the bear was probably miles away by then, and that they would wait right where they were while he looked around. He was only gone a minute or two when they heard him scream, "**BEAR!**" He came running back to the patrol thoroughly shaken having seen Whitepatch not far away.

Sure enough, they caught glimpses of Whitepatch coming warily towards them through the small maples which were thick in that spot. The bear was behaving very strangely, pacing back and forth as it kept coming in closer and closer to the patrol. The patrol members decided that they were being stalked by this bear, and they prepared to shoot it. It kept coming in closer and closer until it was no more than fifteen feet away. Then they got a clear view of the bear and shot him. They did not waste their opportunity of ridding the park of such a fearless and dangerous beast; a beast which was created by people feeding him. This sad affair can be blamed on all those people who had ever fed Whitepatch. **NEVER** feed any bear!

IT'S UNBEARABLY EMBEARRASSING

Back in about 1979, Ranger Don Harris and I had an interesting experience. It involved a large bear which had been hanging around the Lake of the Clouds scenic area and nearby picnic areas. This big bear was tall and lanky, not fat. The bear had become so much of a pest that it was necessary to try and trap it. It had started regular raids of the trash barrels at the above locations, and it was hoped that a little relocation would get it off of the garbage diet and free up our staff to do other things than picking up trash.

A bear live trap is actually just a large culvert sized piece of steel tubing with a vertically sliding door on one end. The other end has a steel mesh grating, a small door for baiting, and a lever from the top connecting the bait pail inside to a cable outside. The cable leads back to a spring loaded pin, which holds the door up when set and locks the door after it drops. The traps are from 32 to 36 inches in diameter and 8 feet long. Some may be larger. The idea is for the bear to go in and grab the bait pail, thereby releasing the door and locking itself inside.

These traps work quite well, and we had little difficulty in catching this particular bear. The only problem was in keeping him in the trap. These live traps are mobile. They are actually a trailer with wheels permanently mounted on each side about in the middle. There is a trailer hitch attached to a tongue on the grating end of the trap. Don and I went to pick up the trap after being informed that we had caught the bear. It is a little nerve wracking trying to connect the tongue of the trap to the trailer ball on a pickup truck's bumper. The problem here is that the bear, which has been in the trap for who knows how long - perhaps all night - is not very happy about being in it. Unhappy bear are no fun to be around at all. They growl, they whine, they hiss, they pop their mouths open and shut, and do other annoying things which can upset those, such as myself, who have to be around them in situations like this.

As soon as anyone tries to pick up the tongue of the trap to connect it to the truck, the bear charges them. It takes nerves of steel not to jump when this occurs. I have never met anyone with nerves of steel yet. The grating on the tongue end of the trap appears none too sturdy when a violently furious 200+ pound bear throws all of its weight against it. Imagine leaning over with your shoulder a few inches from this steel grating. The bear charges you, growling and hissing, bashing into the grate, sloshing you with saliva, and all you can see are teeth and claws sticking out at you through the grates a few inches away. Also, there is the terrible sound of the bear chewing and clawing at the steel grate trying to get at you. Well, the grating always holds up, and the trap always gets hooked up eventually. In more recent years a remedy for this ranger problem has been discovered. Simply putting a heavy cloth over the grating while working nearby results in the bear remaining much more calm.

Don and I finally recovered from the initial shock of the first attempt to grab ahold of the tongue of the trap. The bear had charged, we had jumped back, and now having recovered we were braced for the next attempt. We grabbed the tongue, pulled and lifted, but the tongue would not rise up at all. We had forgotten to remove the blocks which hold up the door end of the trap, and prevent the grating end from rising off the ground. So we knocked the blocking out from under the door end and returned to the front of the trap where the bear was waiting for us behind the grating. We grabbed the tongue again and lifted, but the bear pulled one of those really neat and quick bear tricks that surprised us. Just then, instead of charging us, he ran to the back of the trap. This caused the tongue of the trap to shoot up into the air as the back end banged on the ground from the weight of the bear. As soon as the rear of the trap hit the ground, the door started popping up and down as the bear tried to lift it with his paws. We both ran back to try and hold the door down, but it kept popping up more and more each time as the bear discovered how to get a better paw on it.

I realized it was useless to hold the door down with our hands against an angry bear, so I tried to get the locking pin to go into place. Meanwhile, Don was still trying to hold the sliding steel door down. I could not get the pin to move, so I ran for the truck door yelling for Don to do the same. The last two times the door popped up, Don's hands were thrown up over a foot. Then he gave up and ran for the truck. I just got my door shut as I heard the loud bang of the trap door slamming down, and I caught a good view in the mirror of a big bear disappearing fast into the woods.

All of the action parts of this occurrence happened within 10 or 15 seconds - not much time to think. What a way to get your adrenalin pumping! I just happen to have lots of gray hair, and now you probably know why. After allowing our blood pressure to come back down a little, we checked the trap to see why the door was not locked. The spring loaded mechanism was not working and had not been working when the trap was set, we found out later.

In all probability, the bear was as frightened as we were. I think it had such an unpleasant experience in the trap that it left the area because we did not have problems with the trash barrels caused by that bear afterwards.

THE HEAVY BEARS

The average size of the problem bears which the rangers usually deal with at Porcupine Mountains Wilderness State Park is around 125 to 150 pounds. The bears which get hooked on human food or park garbage always lose their fear of man, and sooner or later they get themselves into trouble. Then it becomes necessary to destroy them in order to protect the people who are utilizing the park. Another thing which happens to bears which lose their fear of man is that they are much more likely to be taken by hunters during the hunting season. They are not wary of people at all and sometimes walk right up to amazed hunters. That is what happened to Boo Boo the bear at the end of the summer season in 1985 (see *Outrageous Fortune*). For bears to be able to get really large, they have to live to be a little older than most problem bears get.

There have been some fairly large bears which became problems at the park, but not many. The big male bear, Bruno, at Mirror Lake was around a 250 pounder. He had been around the lake for several years and usually kept his distance, but he eventually started losing all fear and came right up to people. This is not to suggest that large bear will not tear up a camp for food when they come across one. Generally, such large bear avoid men and do not seek out camping areas to hang around for food.

One of the very largest bear I ever saw was from quite a distance away in the early 1970's. I was riding a motorcycle from Copper Harbor to Ironwood and saw this bear crossing highway M-28 near the Wakefield dump. I was on the flat stretch just east of Jackson Creek heading west, and the bear was crossing from south to north near the dump entrance road, which was about half a mile ahead on the highway. It lumbered across the road fairly slowly. I could hardly believe my eyes because it appeared to me that it took up one whole lane of the highway from the tip of its nose to its rump. I was sort of worried about proceeding on my way, but I did. When I came up out of the creek valley, the bear was nowhere in sight. Later that year during the hunting season, the state record bear was taken near the Wakefield dump, which was undoubtedly the bear that I had seen earlier in the year. As I recall it weighed in around 540 pounds after being dressed out, so it was probably around 600 pounds alive. This is an enormous size for a black bear.

I got a fairly close look at a truly huge bear in Porcupine Mountains Wilderness State Park in July of 1984. I was driving a park truck from the Union Bay end of the park to the Presque Isle Scenic Area on the west end of the park. Along South Boundary Road approximately four miles from Presque Isle a mammoth black bear ran across the road 30 yards in front of me. This occurred midday on a sunny day. The shape of this bear was very reminiscent of that of a polar bear. It was very long and **BIG**. It literally was as long as one of the road lanes is wide. South Boundary Road has ten foot wide traffic lanes, and that is how long this bear was from tip of nose to the other end.

There was another huge bear which came to my attention while I was motoring around on my cycle back in the early 1970's. There was a lot of exploring to be done around the Keweenaw area, which I was new to. On one trip over to the Bete Gris and Lac La Belle area, I happened by the Bette Gris dump. No sooner had I turned in to the dump entrance road than I was startled to be staring at an enormous bear only about 30 yards away. This bear was shaped a lot like a pear, and was obviously very fat and well fed. It was **huge**! I would estimate its weight at around 450 to 500 pounds. This was back when I was relatively new to bear country. Rushing to turn around my cycle as fast as possible to get out of there, the cycle stalled. I then pushed the cycle back out onto the road. Did you ever have a dream where you were trying to do something as fast as possible, but you could only move very slowly? That is how I felt in this situation, but it was no dream.

My very first bear sighting occurred on the second or third night after I moved to Porcupine Mountains State Park in 1970. I was staying in park quarters affectionately called the Black Shack. This structure at that time was unfinished on the inside, and often we had bats flying around inside at night. One night when all the other rangers were out and just as I was going to hit the sack, I looked out of my window towards the garage just across the driveway. It was brightly moonlit outside, and I noticed something moving near the far end of the garage. It was a bear - a big bear, probably around 400 pounds. The bear walked slowly around the garage towards me, came right up underneath the windows of the blackshack, and then meandered off towards the Carpenter Shop. I was mortified. The flimsy glass in the windows would never stop such a creature if he wanted in, and I could even imagine him crashing down the door on the building.

When the other rangers returned to the quarters, I told them about the huge bear. I must have really made an impression upon them because one of them, John Bezotte, brought back a rifle the next time he went home, just in case. He also brought back a BB pistol for the bats.

My wife and I came across a quite large bear in 1973 while we were on a beach near Keweenaw Point. We drove as far out on the old logging roads as we could go by motorcycle, and then walked a mile or two from there. We were at a spot which had an all gravel beach about 30 feet wide, with a foot and a half drop from the woods edge down to the gravel. While I was busy looking around at my feet, I heard her come running up behind me yelling in a whisper, "Bear, a bear." I turned towards her and looked up to see her jumping up and down and repeating it, "Bear, bear." I could not understand why she had stopped back about 15 feet from me, but then it occurred to me. I could tell by her eyes being so big that the bear must be right behind me. I quickly looked around, but no bear there. Whew!

I asked her where the bear was, and she pointed back down the beach from where she had come. No bear there - wait, yes there was. Here came a **big** bear out from the woods just then. It slowly put its front paws down on the beach and then plunked down its rear end. I would now estimate it was around 400 pounds. It was about 50 feet away and just sniffing around, and it didn't seem to notice we were there at all. My wife suggested that we throw our little carry bag, which had some snacks in it, to the bear. I said no. I looked around for some kind of weapon and for some place to retreat to. There was a lot of driftwood around, so I selected a clublike post which fit my hand the best, and we went out on a ridge of rock which extended out a little into the lake.

I did not like this situation at all. Here we were, miles from anywhere, with no weapon of any kind except my club, and just a few yards from a very large bruin. It still was not aware that we were nearby. When my wife first noticed the bear, she had heard the snap of a twig in the woods, which she attributed to a chipmunk. On looking for the chipmunk, she clearly saw this monster black bear moving between the trees and took off to let me know. In order to get back to our transportation, we had to get back down the shoreline on the other side of the bear. What would you do in this situation?

Well, what I decided to do worked well enough. I got all ready out on the rocks with my club, and I summoned up the best Tarzan yell that I could muster: "A-Ah-A-Ah-A-Ah," then I yelled, "Get outa here!" as loud as I could. The bear was startled, looked around our way, and took off into the woods. We waited awhile out on the rocks and then, club in hand, quickly went back to my motorcycle and left.

Here is another example of a gibungous black bear from the Copper Country. (Copper Country refers to the copper mining district of the western Upper Peninsula of Michigan. It extends from Copper Harbor down the Keweenaw Peninsula to the Porcupine Mountains area.) Bob Hill, the award winning bear trapping assistant manager of Fort Wilkins State Park (see *From Copper Harbor With Love*) set a trap at the Harbor Haus Restaurant in Copper Harbor to catch a problem causing bruin. This was back in 1985. The bruin was actually caught several times, but someone kept releasing it from the trap. After quite a few tries, the bear was finally in the trap when he checked it one time.

This bear was so large that it barely would fit inside the trap. Bob and the Conservation Officer involved could see no light around the bear in the trap. It had actually squeezed into the trap in order to get the bait. This bear was so unusually large that they decided to weigh it at a truck scale. The bear weighed 635 pounds! No, this is not a misprint. Yes, the bear weighed in at 635 pounds. I used to think that a 250 pound bear in a livetrap was a lot of bear.

I can just imagine all the hikers, campers, backpackers and cabin users who are somewhere out in the woods right now stopping and saying to themselves, "635 pounds? There are bears in Michigan that weigh 635 pounds? What am I doing here?" Well, relax; bears which are *that* big don't get that way by picking on people.

MISCELLANEOUS BEARS

STANDING BEARS

Why do bears sometimes stand up on their rear legs? To get a better view, and possibly to intimidate enemies. The bear, which Jim Richardson almost ran right into (see *She Was The Terror Of The Porkies*), stood up when it heard him running across the bridge towards it. This was probably done for both of the above reasons. Similarly, the bear Dan Castle was chasing (or should we say following while clanking tools together?) stood up to look back at him.

One nice sunny summer day a large bear was standing just at the edge of the woods along M-26 not far from Greenland, Michigan. It appeared to be checking for traffic. The driver of the passing vehicle wanted to get a picture of it standing there so he stopped just past the bear. But the bear went back into the woods as soon as the vehicle stopped.

There were two large bears standing next to each other along South Boundary Road in the Porkies one summer evening in 1986. It was just at dusk. From a distance they appeared to be two backpackers, with their packs sticking high into the air. Upon closer view, it was two bears which were looking directly at each other. As soon as the vehicle got within 75 yards of them, they stood down and ran into the woods. Perhaps another reason they stand up is to court or to bluff other bears.

Bears also stand up to be able to reach higher. They like to claw at soft wood, often leaving extensively clawed areas on trees or posts. These may be territorial markers. There is a very impressive display of claw marks on a large red pine tree on the Overlook Trail in Porcupine Mountains. The tree is about one mile from the south end of the trail. The marks are about 9 feet high on the tree trunk.

There was also an impressive set of claw marks on top of the old entrance sign on the west end of the Porkies. There was a horizontal top timber about 8 feet above the ground. When this was being stained, the author discovered that the top of it was thoroughly covered with claw marks.

RUNNING BEARS

If you are ever out in the forest and hear something like a locomotive crashing off through the woods away from you, it is probably a bear that you have startled.

A bear was once released from a DNR live trap at a roadside park near Bete Grise, Michigan. One of the releasing rangers took a movie of the bear as it took off across the road at an angle and ran into the brush on the other side. On film all he had was 4 seconds of black streak. Bears can really move!

Once there was a young bear at the old Porkies dump. A new ranger whom we shall not name (but his initials were D.E.Y.) was sent there to dump the garbage off a two ton truck. When he arrived, a bear appeared to be waiting for garbage. It would not get far enough away for the new ranger to feel comfortable about getting out of the truck and untying the tarp. So the ranger had left the door open, in case a retreat was necessary, while he hugged the truck bed and untied the tarp. This was not easy because he would not take his eyes off the bear for one second.

Eventually he got the tarp off and dumped the garbage. The bear was almost jumping up and down for joy - finally, some food. But the load sort of stuck in the truck bed, and it all released at once. It came thundering down with such a crash that it startled the bear, and he tore off into the woods. The bear's speed was amazing. The temporary absence of the bear gave the ranger ample time to get out and make sure the truck bed was empty.

Then there was the sow with two cubs which tore up the car at Lake of the Clouds parking lot. While she and her cubs were cleaning the food out of the car's trunk via the rear fender, a single bear approached. The car was parked near the pit toilets' location. There were people watching the bears from the parking lot and from near the pit toilets. When the intruding single bear, which had one floppy ear, was just about 30 yards away and directly in front of the trail to the pit toilets, the sow let out a growl and spun around. As the cubs darted up a nearby tree, the sow went after the intruding bear. The intruding bear spun around and ran down the pit toilet path with the sow chasing right after it.

The onlookers did not have time to get out of the bears path. These bears were going full tilt, and both went within a few feet of some of the tourists who were watching from the pit toilet area. The sow chased the single bear on down the hill out of sight and came trotting back up a minute or so later. She returned to the car and proceeded to remove more food from the trunk with the assistance of her cubs. It is most interesting how this bear completely accepted and ignored the presence of humans, but immediately chased another bear away.

JEWEL OF THE CARP

One of the most beautiful sights I have ever seen involved a bear. It was a warm and sunny fall day back in the late 1970's, and I was working at the Lake of the Clouds booth selling vehicle permits. Back then, the permit booth was located in the middle of the north parking lot at the Lake of the Clouds Scenic Area. From the booth, one could look east towards the entrance of the scenic area parking lot and have an excellent view due to the break in the tree line. Through this break the next hill to the east was visible, with other hills which make up the escarpment all in a line into the distance beyond that one, and all had blazing fall foliage.

Each of these hills has a steep cliff face towards the Carp River Valley and has some towering pines which set the hills apart from the rest of the forested landscape. At the end of the parking lot there are many oak trees, and due to the extra sunlight at that opening, the branches of some grow well out over the entrance. These made a natural frame for this beautiful picture of the cliffs, forest, hills, pines and sky. On this occasion, I noticed a small bear cub far out on a high oak branch trying to reach acorns. The cub was out as far on the branch as it could possibly go without the branch bending down and dumping the cub off. It kept reaching and stretching with one paw trying to grasp or knock down more tasty acorns for itself.

A CUTE BEAR

What a terrible shame it was that I did not have a camera handy that day. I informed several tourists that there was a bear in sight, but no one was particularly interested. I have never seen a more beautiful or interesting subject for a nature photograph. If you are ever around Lake of the Clouds in the fall, check out the oak tree tops for bear cubs after acorns.

RANGER'S NOTES

THE BEAR FACTS
Ranger's Bear Incident Notebook entries for 1984
[Items in brackets were added by the author.]

6-30-84 3:00 P.M. Greenstone Falls: Group of 6 girlscouts were wading in the river when 3 bears (sow, yearling & cub) got into their food pack. They tore the pack up & wouldn't leave till the food was gone. Mike.

7-7-84 Food sack swiped in the Shining Cloud Falls area. Bear is suspected, (Footprints found in area), but was not seen. Campers had to leave interior early as all of their food was gone.

7-8-84 Numerous reports of bear encounters coming back from the Mouth of the Big & Little Carp Rivers. Also tales of garbage buried at both these locations. Mike.

7-12-84 Just outside Park Headquarters. A bear climbed into the back of employee's truck while he was in the office. He got into garbage in the truck & refused to be chased away. Manager came to rescue. Chased bear away with car. Mike.

7-14-84 9:45 P.M. Union Bay Campground Office - While this is a "mere" sighting it may be of note: Our "Ski Hill" bear has been hanging around the entrance road to the campground. He was spotted by visitors & the ranger as well (this bodes ill). Mike.

7-14-84 Early in the pre-dawn hours between Toledo Creek & Big Carp River. Camper heard snuffing noise then something bit him on the shoulder right through the tent. (An incident report was filled out). The camper, a wildlife biologist, believes it was a bear. Mike.

7-84 Bear encountered at junction of Correction Line Trail and Big Carp River Trail. Made off with gorp. No real problems - stayed away from people - Whistle not effective.

7-24-84 L.O.C. [Lake of the Clouds] Bridge. Possible bear incident. Bear took food from hanging pack. Claw marks on tree. (Very suspicious).

8-13-84 10:30 A.M. at Shining Cloud Falls. Packing up in A.M. when a 2 year old bear came into camp, ignored the yells of protest, and dragged pack off into woods. Ate a few items & then left.

8-16-84 Packer returning from Big Carp area notified C.G.O. [Campground Office] that bear was in the back of a park visitor's pick up (parked at Little Carp River Road) tearing a cooler to bits. They tried to chase it away, but it would not be distracted from the cooler.

Nobody mentioned this. During July our MCC [Michigan Civilian Conservation Corps] crew lost their lunches (before eating them) to a bear at the Little Carp River Road. Seems they left the van door open. (Bears-1, MCC-0).

8-22-84 Greenstone Falls/Section 17 area. Bears (plural) are very active, reported several hikers leaving early. They get into food and also bite into tents! Mike.

9-22-84 Bear stole food about 1 mile N.E. of the Big Carp River in the afternoon.

PART II: NEW BEAR TALES

Additional Stories, Some Recent, Some Old

WHERE THE BEARS ARE

THE LAST OF THE BEAR PITS

As noted in the introduction, the dumps of the Upper Peninsula were usually marked on the tourist maps as bear pits because bears could often be found in them in the evening. The last bear pit was closed in November of 1990 at Copper Harbor. It was the most famous (or infamous) of all western Upper Peninsula dumps.

The dump was located off of U.S. 41 out the road to Lake Manganese and the Clark Mine. A narrow side road went into the dump which was arranged for bear viewing. The garbage was mounded up in the center of the dump area, and there was driving and parking around the outside of this. Thus, cars could surround the garbage (and bears) in the evening and all shine their lights onto the bears.

While there generally is not a lot of traffic congestion in the Upper Peninsula, often there was plenty of it near the Copper Harbor dump on summer evenings. On any given night there were from five to ten bears and 50 or more cars of onlookers trying to get into and out of a relatively small area on a one lane road.

DOES THE PRESENCE OF BEARS
CAUSE TEMPORARY INSANITY?

Barb Foley of the Country Village Shops in Copper Harbor told me a rather shocking dump story. A grandfather took his two small grandchildren to the Copper Harbor dump to see the bears. He had his camera with him for some pictures of the bruins. While at the dump he got the great idea of getting a picture of the kids sitting on top of a bear's back. It would make a great picture, right?

You guessed it - he actually attempted to place one of the kids on the back of a bear. Luckily, the bear simply ran off as the child was set upon it. The child fell to the ground, fortunately unhurt. This incident could easily have ended as an injury case if not worse. Now you have some idea of why I made a reference to the old bear pit being infamous. The residents and merchants of Copper Harbor were continually on edge about all the possible strange things that the tourists might be doing out at the dump. There was always the possibility that someone might get hurt there.

THE COPPER HARBOR TASTE TEST

Tish Boost of the Gas Lite General Store in Copper Harbor passed along an unusual tale from the old dump. It seems that there was a rather interesting taste comparison of peanut butter brands conducted by two young men utilizing the bears at the Copper Harbor dump a few years ago. They obtained Jif and Peter Pan brands of peanut butter, went to the dump, and liberally spread their test materials over the front bumper and hood of a compact car, Jif on one side, Peter Pan on the other. Then they sat in the car to see what would happen.

Well, as usual with bears, things really started to happen which the two young men had not foreseen at all. A large bear approached their vehicle and started cleaning off the peanut butter. It liked it so much, the bear climbed up onto the hood of the car. The two guys began to worry about the bear pushing in the windshield. This was a smallish car, and the bear was much too heavy for the hood. The hood was permanently dented as well as being scratched up.

The next day the young men went to the Gas Lite General Store for help in washing off the car. This is how Tish found out about the incident. She chastised the two young men for doing something they knew they should not have. But not wanting their misfortune to be an entirely wasted effort, she made sure to find out which brand of peanut butter the bear preferred. It was Jif!

FROM COPPER HARBOR WITH LOVE

It was anticipated that after the closure of the Copper Harbor dump in November, 1990 that there would be a marked increase in bear problems around Copper Harbor during the summer of 1991. This anticipation was not expended in vain. There were numerous problems in 1991; cases of bears entering porches (in one screen, out another); entering cars (in one open window, grab candy and out another open window); into screen tents (in one side, out another); looking into windows; looking into tents; looking into trailers; etc. On one particular occasion a large bear wandering through the Fort Wilkins campground in the evening decided to stop near the toilet building entrance and sit down for awhile. There were three or four campers trapped inside the building who wanted to get out but were afraid to go out past the bear. And who knows how many people were needing to get in to the bathroom?

The presence of bears in the campground at night was not a new phenomenon. The bears had regular rounds through the campground back in the early 1970's when the author used to work up there. Back then they occasionally got into a camper's food or trash. Once they got into a Boy Scout troop's trailer full of food. Another time a bear pawed at the bottom of a motor home door which is rather unusual (something must have smelled good). The campers usually did not notice the bears because the campers were sitting around their fires with their eyes accustomed to the light. The bears were quiet, they were black, and it was dark out. If seen, they were usually seen as a partial silhouette, and it was assumed that they were a camper's dog. There was a sow with cubs that I saw on a couple occasions under these circumstances. You could hear the children talking about the possibility of a bear being around, and hear their parents assuring them that what they probably saw was a dog. It wasn't a dog. The kids were right.

The situation in 1991 was quite different. The bears were not spending most of their time at the Copper Harbor dump as in the past. A relatively large number of bears which had formerly congregated at the dump now spread out to find easy pickings. What easier pickings than the food of campers? Some bears started spending a lot more time around the Fort Wilkins campgrounds. Others headed for the garbage dumpsters of nearby resorts and restaurants.

With all of the problems which resulted from the bears expulsion from the dump, it became necessary to trap many bears in the Copper Harbor area in 1991. Bob Hill, assistant manager of Fort Wilkins State Park, spent a lot of his time setting and baiting the D.N.R. live traps around the area that summer. By summer's end in 1991, a total of 16 bears had been trapped.

We usually think of Copper Harbor as a source of good souvenirs of the Copper Country, not as a source of problem bears. So where did all of these bears get moved to? Well, be assured that they were hauled well south of Houghton into uninhabited forest areas where they could live without causing problems. Hopefully, they all stayed in the areas where they were relocated.

The Copper Harbor Improvement Association presented Bob Hill with a "Bear Pit" award in honor of his efforts at trapping the bears. He had received such an award once before when he removed a bear from the Fort Wilkins State Park store back in 1985 (see *Like a Bull in a China Shop.*)

GOTCHA!

There was one problem bear trapping situation which was a little out of the ordinary for Bob Hill in 1991. He and Conservation Officer Leo Erickson had to set a second trap at the Larry Binford home in Agate Harbor because a sow was trapped on October 3, 1991, but her three cubs were not. In an attempt to get the three cubs into a trap, it was decided to use the mother bear as bait.

To accomplish this, an empty trap was set for the cubs so they would have to enter it to see mama bear. The empty trap was put in line with the trap containing their mother. The grating ends were together as close as possible and the trap door ends out. Due to the tongues of the traps, there was still a large space between the two traps where the cubs could get close to mama without entering the trap. That area was covered with heavy rags so the cubs had to enter the second trap to see mama. The trap for the cubs was set to be manually released by use of a rope. When the cubs entered, the rope was pulled by Mr. Binford, who was having the bear problem. This assured that all the cubs got into the trap and were not injured by the trap door. This worked like a charm.

Then it was necessary that all the bears be transferred into one trap together prior to being moved and released in a remote corner of Baraga County. The transfer was accomplished by putting the two traps end to end next to each other with the doors together. Then both doors were carefully raised so the bears could get together. It was expected that the cubs would try to get into the mother's trap. What happened was that the mother squeezed through the opening in her door when it was only about eight inches high to get into the trap with her cubs. Love knows no bounds!

A NIGHT TO REMEMBEAR

Merle Audette of the Union River Campground in Porcupine Mountains Wilderness State Park told me of a motorcyclist who had a problem at the Copper Harbor dump in 1988. He had camped at her facility, and had showed her the evidence of his story. The cyclist had made the required evening pilgrimage to the Copper Harbor dump while in town. He even went prepared with some goodies to feed to the bears. When he arrived at the dump, he watched what was going on for awhile before shutting off his machine. Having determined that he could toss his goodies to the bears with no danger to himself, he opened a can of pop, drank part of it, set it on his motorcycle seat, and then took his treats over towards the bears. When he came back to his bike, a bear had grabbed the rest of his pop. It had also bitten into the seat of his Honda Gold Wing. I hate it when that happens!

1992

There had already been bear problems up in Keweenaw County prior to April 17, 1992. Bob Hill informed me on that date that a bear had entered a window on the metal trash transfer building used to contain and store the trash of the area towns for reshipment to a licensed landfill. The bruin entered one window and exited through another, as usual. Bob, winner of two previous "Bear Pit" awards was preparing to trap the culprit, and start working early toward a possible third award for the summer 1992 bear problem season.

THE BEAR AT THE END OF THE RAINBOW

In 1990 there was one especially large boar which hung around Silver City, Michigan. It weighed around 250 pounds and kept raiding the trash at the End of the Rainbow Restaurant and at the Union River Private Campground. It became so bold that it was walking right up to people in the campground. Prior to its capture, the bruin had been wandering around the campground taking coolers from campsites. It would growl at the campers if they were in its way.

The Porkies staff were asked to try and trap this bear. I happened to be the one on duty after it was caught. When hooking up the trap to the truck, I used the new method of covering the hitch/grating end of the trap so the bear could not see me and attempt to tear the grating out of the trap to get at me. But I could not lift the trap because the bear was right at the front. I had to get Norm Audette, the operator of the private campground, to help. Together we had no problem lifting the tongue of the trap and hooking it up to the truck. This bear was taken well over towards the Huron Mountains for release. However, one of the bears which is already hanging around in the Silver City area this year is quite large according to Don Harris. It might be the same bear hauled away two years ago. Bear have often been known to return from great distances after being trapped and hauled away.

The new bear pit in the Silver City / Porkies Park area is the garbage dumpster behind the End of the Rainbow Restaurant in Silver City, Michigan. It is now the new evening gathering spot for bears who wish to find garbage, and for tourists who wish to see bears. A couple of bear have already been hanging around there as of the first week in May, 1992. Unfortunately for the operators of the restaurant, the bears cause all kinds of trash problems.

Usually the bears will not eat right at the dumpster. Instead, they come out of the surrounding woods and grab a bag of trash which they then drag back into the woods to tear up. Many times I have driven by in the morning going to work and seen a tremendous amount of trash strewn here and there behind the restaurant. The bears have even developed a more heavily used trail straight back behind the dumpster where they enter and leave the woods. After the bear has been active, this trail stands out markedly because it is paved with trash and plastic bags.

THEY SHOOT BEARS, DON'T THEY?

STOP THIEF

Porcupine Mountains Wilderness State Park has 13 older cabins rented out from spring through fall, and three additional brand new cabins rented out year round. One of the latter, called Whitetail Cabin, is located on a winter cross country ski trail called the Deer Yard Trail. This is because the trail runs through a winter yarding area for deer.

Now, like it or not, the Porkies are open to hunting during the fall and winter seasons. Firearm deer hunting season is from November

15th through the 30th. Just about the only people utilizing the park at that time of year are the deer hunters themselves. The last two weeks in November, which coincides with the Michigan firearm deer season, is just about the time of year that bear usually go into their winter dens. This is also the time of year when snow usually starts accumulating on the ground.

In 1991 a rather unusual incident occurred during the deer season at the new Whitetail Cabin according to Paulette Aho, the Park Secretary, and Sandy Perez, the Park Communications Clerk. Six deer hunters had rented the cabin for the firearm deer season. Two of them had been successful bagging an 8 point buck and another smaller deer. Three of the hunters were at the cabin discussing the size of the 8 point buck's rack when a fourth hunting party member returned to the cabin with a 4 point buck. He left his kill just outside the door of the cabin and entered in the middle of the discussion about the large buck's antlers. By now it was quite dark outside, so when it was decided to go out and examine the 8 pointer's rack, flashlights were necessary to see. Out into the cabin yard, the four deer hunters went with flashlights to examine the larger deer's antlers. As they aimed their lights onto the dear head, it was difficult to get a clear look at the antlers. They were twisting around even though it was not windy at all.

The hunters naturally aimed their lights down a little lower on the deer carcass and, lo and behold, there was not much of a deer carcass left to look at. In fact, there was a good sized bear right in the process of eating the deer while the men watched. The bruin had already eaten most of the hind quarters and was working on the rib areas when discovered. The hunters immediately chased the bear away. Then they hauled the partially eaten carcass and the two other deer to be secured in the back of a pickup truck with a topper on it. The following day the hunters took the two and a half deer to park headquarters to be measured for their deer hunter patches.

YOUNG HUNTERS CAN'T JUMP

There was a case in Northern Wisconsin in the late 1980's where a bear hunter was "forced" out of a tree stand by a sow black bear with cubs. The hunter was a 14 year old girl who was apparently bow hunting for bear from a tree stand. She had baited an area below her stand and had taken the rest of the bait into the stand with her. She saw the bear with two cubs heading her way. Sows with cubs are not fair game. The sow ate the young hunter's bait and then went up into the tree stand for the rest of it. Somehow the girl ended up being forced out of the tree stand. Whether she jumped or was knocked or pushed out is not clear. She was knocked unconscious upon hitting the ground. When she awoke, the bear and cubs were gone. The young hunter was not otherwise injured by the sow.

PAW OF FURY

There was an incident involving major injury to a bear hunter in the Marenisco area in about 1982. The hunter was utilizing a bait to attract bear, and was standing next to a deadfallen tree which extended back about forty feet behind him. He heard a noise at the far end of the windfall and shot a bear he saw there. It turned out to be a cub. Suddenly, the mother bear came running around the other end of the deadfall. The hunter got two shots off at the sow hitting it in the chest and rear leg. Unfortunately for him, the mother bear was not immediately killed. She proceeded to inflict numerous severe bite marks to the hunter's face, arm and leg. After the hunter was still, the mortally wounded sow left to die in the woods.

The hunter managed to get out of the woods and back to his hunting buddies. They went back to the scene of the incident the following day and were able to locate the mother bear. She was still alive, although nearly dead. The injured hunter's buddies also found another cub with the sow. They killed both bears. Possibly the sow had attacked the hunter so furiously in order to protect her second cub. The hunter required extensive stitches (I heard several hundred) and plastic surgery.

SOMETHING WILD

Don Harris and Loren Niemi of Silver City had an unusual encounter in the Porkies in 1980. On the opening day of bear season, they were going into a trailless area to bait for bear. Don and Loren were carrying packs full of bear bait. Exactly what it was is a secret - sorry. However, you can be assured that bears liked whatever it was. Don and Loren walked back almost two miles from the nearest road. As they approached the bait area, which they had baited previously a few days before, they saw a bear.

This bear did not run away as bears in such situations usually do. Instead it came towards them. Don described the bear as stalking them. He talked to the bear, but it kept coming towards them. Then he yelled at the bear, but it kept coming towards them. He turned to Loren, but he had dropped his pack and climbed a tree already. Don had a bear hunting license and a short barreled shotgun with buckshot in it which he now prepared to use. He did not want to shoot the bear, because he was baiting for other hunters, and had the gun only for defense. Don yelled again, but the bear kept coming. The bear was now less than twenty yards away and still slowly approaching. So Don knelt down, carefully aimed right at the bear's head, and fired.

The bear instantly halted with a jerking movement and laid its ears back, then it turned and ran away. Don could not believe that he had missed, but he had not hit the bear except for one pellet grazing one of its ears. The bear was easily identified after that time because one of its ears was floppy. The floppy eared bear hung around the Lake of the Clouds area for the following six years. In 1981 it was often at the Lake of the Clouds parking lot in the summer. In fact, it was the single bear which the sow chased through the people near the pit toilets (see *Risky Business*).

BRUINAPHOBIA!

In a September 17, 1987 article from the Daily Mining Gazette (Houghton, Michigan) is a description of an encounter between a local bear hunter, Kim Stoker, and a bear family on the opening day of the bear hunting season. Kim was just leaving his hunting spot. He turned to check out a noise and turned back to be nose to nose with a bear cub. It let out a squeal and ran for a tree with a sibling. Suddenly, the sow was directly in front of him. She stood up, roared, charged, retreated and repeated this sequence of events several times, each time stopping a little further away from Kim.

This occurred quickly. Kim tried to get his gun into position while he backed away from the sow. The sow was making her threatening charges and retreats, but was basically doing the same thing Kim was - that is, backing away. Kim was not interested in shooting a sow with cubs. They both backed away far enough that they were able to disengage from possible hostilities. Kim was happy to have been able to get out of that situation without damage to either himself or the bears.

A little excitement helps keep one's life values in order.

ESCAPE FROM PORCUPINE MOUNTAINS

Usually the author finds out about bear incidents which occur at Porcupine Mountains from other rangers while at work. This incident was different. My wife told me about it at home on my day off when she got back from shopping in "downtown" Ontonagon. She heard about it from a lady while at the St. Vincent de Pauls store there. The lady had heard about it while at Syl's Restaurant in Ontonagon. The person it had happened to early in the day was telling everyone who would listen all about it a few hours later at Syl's Restaurant.

Joan Peterson from Green Bay had camped at White Pine Extension Outpost Campground in Porcupine Mountains Wilderness State Park. At 6:30 the next morning a bear was hanging around her campsite. It attempted to get into her car. It climbed onto the hood of her 1980 Ford Escort. It also climbed on the trunk. It attempted to open her trunk, tearing off one of the rear taillight covers and license plate in the process.

Needless to say, Joan, camped alone, was not overly pleased about the situation. She was in her flimsy little ol' tent watching a good sized bear try to destroy her car, her only means of escape to safety! The bear went to the driver's side while she watched from her tent with increasing apprehension. The bear forced the driver's side window in and broke it! It had been rolled down a couple of inches. The bear climbed inside and chewed on her headrest and other vinyl covered parts (must have been the hide of nauga, again). It rifled through the food she had stored in her back seat, took a bag of trail mix, and left with it.

Joan must have been in an awful state of mind as she watched the bear damaging her car from her tent. When the bear left with the trail mix, Joan seized the moment! She ran from her tent to the car, hopped in right on top of the glass, started up and got out of there! She sped west towards the Presque Isle Scenic Area where she stopped at the campsite of some friends. Around 8:30 A.M. she reported the incident to Mike Caramella, a summer ranger who was making his rounds registering camps. Mike talked to Joan for around thirty minutes trying to quiet her down as Joan was very, very upset. She explained what had happened, and showed Mike her car. He was quick to notice the bear prints on the hood and trunk area, and the damage to the car indicated above. Mike cleaned the glass out of the car. Joan wanted to retrieve her camping gear and go home, but did not want to go back to White Pine Outpost alone.

Mike suggested she wait in the Presque Isle Campground with her friends until Ranger Don Harris left Presque Isle to go back to the Union Bay end of the Porkies a little later in the morning. That way, Don could stop at White Pine Outpost with her so she could pick up her gear. In the meantime, Joan excitedly told her story to many of the campers in the Presque Isle Campground. When she and Don left Presque Isle an hour later, almost everyone there knew all about the incident.

Don and Joan stopped at White Pine Outpost and retrieved all of Joan's gear. Then they both went east, Don to Union Bay, and Joan to Ontonagon. Joan stopped at Syl's Restaurant prior to noon. She was still very upset and telling everyone around her what had happened to her and how she had escaped.

BEARING THE BRUNT OF THE MEDUSA EFFECT

Randy Bruntjens is a Forest Fire Officer for the Michigan Department of Natural Resources. In the summer of 1991 he was stationed at the Wakefield Fire Station. He went out one nice July day to check on a beaver complaint near the Marenisco area. After parking his truck, he headed down an old railroad grade into an area of thick alder choked lowland.

Randy went down off to the left of the grade into the dense alder of the low lying area to take a closer look at possible beaver problems. It was so thick there that a clear view of anything was almost impossible unless one was standing right on top of it. Suddenly there was a squealing sound, and then a racket in the alders as a small bear cub which Randy had almost stepped on ran off through the dense growth.

Randy decided it might be better to go back to the railroad grade which was behind him. He climbed up and onto the grade where he was met by the sow bear. She was a little further along the grade on the opposite side from him. As soon as he was all the way onto the grade, she rushed at him, stopping only five to seven feet away where she reared up on her back legs. She was popping her mouth, clawing at the air in his direction, and otherwise letting him know she was very upset. Randy made like a statue and just froze in his position facing the bear. His heart was suddenly pounding furiously, and he became very pale. Motionless, Randy just watched and took in all the threats mama bear was dishing out at him.

After what seemed like hours of violent intimidation from the sow, but was probably more like 15 to 30 seconds of this warning behavior, the mother bear stood down and headed away from Randy on the grade. After she was about 50 yards away, Randy decided it was time to get out of there. Keeping his eyes on the bear, he slowly started to turn his body in the other direction.

Unfortunately, Randy dragged his foot in the gravel just enough to make noise which the sow could hear. She turned immediately and ran back to within about 15 feet of him this time. Randy once again turned to stone. This time he was in a pretty awkward position. His head was facing the bear, but his body wasn't. He was sort of in the middle of the turning position with a lot of weight shifted onto one leg, but he did not move!

The bear did not stand up this time. She did make nasty popping noises with her mouth as upset bears are apt to do. Once again after a short while, the bear turned and headed towards the direction the cub had gone. Randy did not attempt to move even though he was not very comfortable. He waited until the bear had gone down the grade aways and turned to the left into the alders. Then he waited until he could not hear the bear making any noise in the alders as she headed away with her cub. Then he waited even a little while longer, just in case. He certainly did not need another dose of adrenalin that day.

After about two or three minutes in the awkward position, Randy finished his turn and quickly went back on the grade towards where his truck was. He did not check on the beaver problem that day. He returned to the Wakefield Fire Station, and at the end of his work day, he went home to Gladsone, Michigan. Hours later, when he arrived at home, his wife quickly noticed that he was as white as a sheet.

Bears have a way of doing that to you!

REPEAT AFTER ME

Don Harris, Porcupine Mountains Ranger, has had more than his share of bear encounters. One of the more exciting happened while working. He was coming out on the Lake Superior Trail from the Buckshot Cabin area. About three quarters of a mile from the cabin he had to crawl under a tree which had fallen on the trail. He was carrying a backpack which made this a little more difficult than it otherwise would be.

In this area there were many small fir trees. As Don shuffled under the tree, he heard something make a noise and run away to his left. On standing up on the other side of the downed tree, he saw a large bear further up the trail on the right side. It was behind a small fir tree. The bear stood up and looked Don's way. Then it went down on all fours and charged full tilt towards Don!

Don threw down his pack and ran for a white birch tree just to his left. He yelled at the bear and climbed quickly up the tree to what he hoped was a safe distance. The bear stopped for a moment when Don yelled, then resumed its charge, stopping only when it got to the tree. This bear was upset. It stood and clawed at the tree, growled and popped its mouth, then stood down on all fours and walked around the tree making menacing noises and looking up at Don.

Don figured out by now that the sound he had heard was a cub, or cubs, running away from near where he had scooted under the downed tree. They were further in that direction making noises now and then. After what seemed like many minutes, but probably was not, the bear backed away from the tree into the thick underbrush. Don waited a few moments and then came down from the tree. His arms were tired as the tree was straight with no footholds. As soon as he hit the ground, the sow bear came rushing out of the brush at him again. He climbed up the tree again, higher this time. In fact, he climbed up as high as he could get.

The bear did not put her paws on the tree this time. She walked around it making all those nasty noises and looking up. Then she left more quickly than the previous time in the same direction. Don waited for several minutes before coming down. Then he picked up his pack and hastened to leave the area.

BEARS, LIES, AND VIDEOTAPE

THE 1989 LILY POND CABIN INCIDENTS

The following story centers around an incident which occurred early in 1989 at the Lily Pond Cabin in Porcupine Mountains Wilderness State Park. After the original incident, subsequent cabin users speculating on the evidence regarding the incident put many comments in the Cabin Log Book. The cabins in the Porkies are all provided with a "Log Book" for the users to enter their comments, observations and tips for others to read.

Park cabins are rented out by the day, and most occupants stay from one to five days. The items below which are preceded by a date are excerpts from the Lily Pond Cabin Log Book for summer 1989. All Log excerpts are by entirely different cabin users unless noted otherwise.

May 29   "...a big black bear came to visit. We tried yelling & pounding on the cabin walls and he just looked at us, even stood up and looked through the windows. Mike tried going outside and yelling and that bear just ran at him (a good lesson here somewhere). Well, that bear pulled on the rope where it was tied to the cabin till it broke where it went over the branch. Even took a chunk out of the back corner there. He grabbed the bag and high tailed it."

June 7   "Do not feed the bears! We just spent a hellish night. About 7:30 P.M. a bear came and we were interested. But then it began to tear siding off the cabin. While that may not sound too awful, our terror seems a perfectly rational response to the situation.

Ticks carrying Lyme disease pale by comparison. We thought we'd done everything as instructed. We put all food in mouseproof containers. We put trash in a plastic bag in the stove. We'd just had dinner and had the door open. Maybe it wanted our freeze dried vegetable stew beef. There's no doubt it was trying to get in - just look at the damage. At least two previous visitors write of setting out food to bring in a bear. DO NOT DO IT. This bear was too used to people. Even the suggested trick of banging pans didn't faze it at all.

We thought of hiking out last night, but hiking in the dark and possibly running [into] this or another bear kept us here. It's now 5:45 A.M. and we're leaving when it gets a bit lighter and we get our courage up. The bear didn't come back after dark, but we surely didn't trust it to be really gone.

So we're leaving a day early. Has it completely ruined our Lily Pond vacation? We'll see when we're safely back in the car."

The two ladies involved want everyone to know, "Do not feed the bears!" They stopped at the park office when leaving the park to report their incident. Those who saw them were impressed by how upset they were. The ladies had taken pictures of the bear and of the damage it had inflicted on the cabin, and sent several color prints to the Park after having their film developed. The park personnel made it a point to show these pictures to subsequent Lily Pond Cabin occupants for a time.

Most later Lily Pond cabin occupants were aware of the cause of the damage to the cabin due to the Log Book entries, and many of them wrote comments of their own concerning the same. Interestingly, some later cabin occupants doubted that a bear had torn the siding off the cabin. They suggested that perhaps the people who had reported the incident had done the damage to get firewood more easily than going out and hunting for it in the woods.

June 30 "Well, we made it in with no sign of the bear."

July 1 "After seeing the pictures of the cabin & the bear at the field office I wasn't sure we should come to Lily Pond. But so far we haven't seen him."
[Note: The park office still has the pictures. If you wish to see them, just ask.]

July 5 "The looks of the side scare the daylights out of me. From the log, I gather the bear has not been around in about a month - hope he stays away tonight. Am wondering whether to leave shutters open tonight. The fresh breeze would be welcome, but I wonder how bear-proof the windows and screens are. I will not do any cooking outdoors - just boil water. Am mad at myself for not asking the ranger this morning if Lily Pond had been having bear trouble and what the current status is. I blew it."

July 6 (Same occupant as the 5th) "The bear visited last night several times - late 11:45 1:15-ish. Scratching at door [&] walls. I'm not staying another night   too scary. Just hope I don't meet up with him on the trail out. Miserable night."

July 22 "We've been here three days now & no sign of the bear. I think someone ripped the siding off the cabin because they didn't want to look further for firewood, & just made up the bear story. Keep it up though. It helps to keep people away."

July 25 "Tonight we started to read the journal and read about the bear attacks. We had been leaving the screen door locked and not using the out side door. Tonight we locked the wooden door and debated about the shutters."

July 26 "After the stories of our friendly bear I was scared but there was no signs of the bear. I did take pictures of the cabin where the bear ate the cabin so when I tell our story it won't look like I am full of s___!"

July 29 "OK - did someone make up all those bear stories or are they real? Why would a bear want to rip boards off the house?"

August 1 "Saw the "Bear" wreckage no <u>claw marks</u> & we think it's vandals."

August 23 "Well so did a bear do that to the cabin? I don't think so. We did see some bear tracks way down the tail."

August 26 "We, too, spent the better part of an hour debating whether a bear had attacked the structure in which we spent the night."

September 12 "We have seen no sign of bear and don't think any of the damage to the outside was from a bear. Most likely from lazy packers too tired to find wood."

September 15 "Frankly, I find the bear story ... pretty hard to swallow."

September 20 "The torn siding looks pretty scary - but are those bear stories really true."

TO ALL THOSE THAT DOUBT

September 28 "To all those that doubt the damage to the cabin was done by a bear, I can assure you it was. My friend and I arrived here on June 17, the date I'm not sure of but we were here the third week of June. We arrived to find the cabin much as it is now. I at first thought it was the work of vandals but after closer examination knew what was to blame. We had been here for less than an hour when my friend felt "nature's call." Having packed in a VCR camcorder, against my better judgment, I went outside to film his journey. When the door closed I shut the camera off and turned to find the bear between the pine stump & cabin door. I ran to the John, where we both stayed and observed him for the next 20 minutes or so. The previous hikers had left food on the stump which we, while unpacking, had not gotten rid of. While I beat on the walls, blew on the whistle, & shouted, he was not at all concerned. After finishing the food he came to the back of the cabin. Standing erect he looked in our direction, then back to the cabin, he then went about his task of ripping more siding from the wall. He did it with little effort, I might add. He then headed off toward the pond & we saw him no more. We did get a couple of good pictures of him on tape..."

The author and Ranger Jim Richardson went to Lily Pond later in the year to remove the rest of the damaged siding and measure for replacement material. We had a very difficult time removing the broken boards and old nails with appropriate tools - hammers, crowbars and superbars. There was plenty of evidence that a bear had torn the siding off of the cabin. There were numerous sets of claw marks, not only on the damaged area, but also other places on the cabin. Additionally, there were numerous bite marks especially at the corners. Many of the park cabins, if not all, have various bear bite and claw markings. Some have even had a piece of siding pulled off before. However, none previously have had a bear tear off almost a fourth of the front and back siding, especially while there were cabin occupants making noise in an effort to scare the bear away.

Bears like to chew soft wood. The park's sign posts used to be made out of cedar. Bears literally devoured them. I still remember two particular ones at the top of Sunset ski run at the Porkies Ski Hill. One was chewed so much that the 4"x4" post was narrowed at one spot about four feet high to about 1"x1". The other was extensively chewed also and had an unusually large knot on a corner edge which resulted in a sharp piece pointing downward. This had a tuft of coarse black hair wedged in under it, a result of bears rubbing against the post.

I have seen signs which could not be read. The edges had been chewed all the way around until there was only a small middle piece of the original sign left. Years ago rangers discovered that if a line of nails sticking out about 1" was put all around the edges of a sign, bears would not chew on it. There may still be some of these old signs in the park. The bears never touched them for some reason. More recently, barbed wire has been attached around the edges of a few of the very large interior signs. This also seems to have deterred the bruins.

Bears like to claw trees, possibly for exercise, possibly for marking territory. As stated elsewhere, many of the huge old Park entrance posts had extensive clawing, and some trees have been found with the same.

SHORT BEAR TALES

DANCES WITH BEARS

Once upon a time there was a good sized bear which had been caught in the Porkies live trap. A ranger, who shall remain anonymous (not D.E.Y.), prepared to mark this pesky bear for future identification. This is sometimes necessary if it is believed that the same bear is being trapped again and again at the same location. By marking the bear it can be instantly recognized as one which caused problems at a particular area previously, and appropriate measures can be taken such as hauling it farther away for release.

As mentioned elsewhere in this book, the live trap consists of a cylindrical steel tube about three feet in diameter and eight feet long with a grating on one end and a vertically sliding door on the other. It is mounted on wheels for transportation, and has a tongue with ball hitch on the grating end.

On this occasion the ranger was preparing to mark the bear with bright yellow paint. The bear was enough of a problem that it was thought necessary to take this precaution. The following occurrences were observed by a mechanic, Jerry Monk, from a nearby garage.

The ranger positioned his pail of paint near the grating end of the trap, which was connected to a pickup truck. He prepared a long pole with a rag wrapped around one end to dip into the paint can. Making sure that the bear had its rear end towards the trap grating, he dipped the rag into the paint and then quickly inserted the long pole into one of the openings. Then he moved the pole further into the trap with the dripping yellow paint directed towards the rear end of the bear. At the same time he made this motion, he moved forward himself and straddled the tongue of the trap with his legs. He was holding the pole to one side as it was longer than necessary and stuck out beyond where he was straddling the tongue and over the tailgate of the truck.

As soon as the ranger jabbed the bear with the dripping yellow paint pole, the bear spun around and grabbed onto the pole with its jaws. The bear then proceeded to jerk the ranger backwards and forwards, up and down, and from side to side. The free end of the pole behind the ranger was flailing wildly around. He was being pushed, pulled, jerked and whacked by the pole, and was sort of holding on for dear life. The ranger didn't quite have this situation under control. Every time the ranger tried to step over the tongue, the bear knocked him off balance and back into the straddling position. Reminds me of a rag doll on a stick.

The ranger was a little shaken and a little wiser, but was not injured.

THE VIEW FROM THE BOTTOM

Long, long ago in a place far, far away, - well, actually it was at Mirror Lake in the Porkies back when the park cabins were built in the 1950's. There used to be another building out in that area. This was used by the park employees who were constructing the cabins as a rest and staging area. According to Al Hanson, a retired carpenter from Porcupine Mountains, one of the workers went into that building after work, laid on the bunk and went to sleep. Shortly afterwards, a bear was seen approaching the open door of the building and entering. It went over to the bunk and sniffed the sleeping worker's feet. The bear then immediately left.

WHERE BEARS DARE

The south side of the Lake of the Clouds, close to the North Mirror Lake Trail bridge has often been used as a camping area by backpackers. Quite a few years ago there was one especially bad problem bear hanging around that area making life miserable for the packers. In one of the incidents, a bear fell on the tent of the backpackers during the night as it was attempting to get at their pack hung directly over their tent. Don't hang your food directly over your tent unless your tent is equipped with hefty truss rafters.

SCARFACE

An unnamed couple camped at the Union River Outpost Campground within Porcupine Mountains State Park in 1971 had what some might consider as a rather harrowing bear encounter. There was a two year old bear which was hanging around that area and bothering campers. As with all such bears, it lost fear of man and became a pesky problem.

One evening the bruin was attracted to the couple's tent for some reason. It could not resist the temptation to enter the tent. It went right in the unsecured tent flaps until it was about halfway inside.

The occupants of the tent were rather startled. The man instinctively grabbed an axe and hit this bear right between the eyes with the sharp blade side of the instrument. The bear left.

Ranger Bill Perrin talked with the campers about the incident. They were not overly excited about it, and in fact, remained camped afterward.

The next time the bear was seen, it was sporting a highly noticeable scar on its face. It remained somewhat of a pest, bearrorizing the Union Bay area for a couple of years, but it **NEVER** went into, or even quite so close to, a tent ever again. The bear was easily recognizable afterwards and was referred to as Scarface.

NIPPED IN THE BUD

Early in the pre dawn hours of July 14, 1984, a backpacker sleeping in his tent between Toledo Creek and the Big Carp River in Porcupine Mountains got a surprise. He woke up and heard sniffing noises outside his tent. Then, without any other warning, something bit him on the shoulder right through the tent. The camper, who was a wildlife biologist from Wisconsin, was not seriously injured.

Ranger George Cameron measured the bite marks left in the tent wall. He and the camper believe that the culprit was a small pesky bear. Thank goodness it wasn't a **BIG** pesky bear!

THE SUMMER OF '88

Ranger Bob Sprague of Porcupine Mountains informed me that he filed numerous bear incident reports in 1988. One of these involved a bear problem at the Mirror Lake area. The report was filed by an uninvolved spectator who witnessed the incident. It seems that a backpacking youth group leader who was clearly having a bad day was seen tugging on one end of a pack and frame while the Mirror Lake bear was tugging on the other end. According to his account, the leader was shouting, "You got one, you're not getting the other pack!"

A SAD BEAR TALE

One sunny early April day in 1988, there were reports from several different skiers of the sighting of a small bear on the side of Copper Run at the Porcupine Mountains Ski Hill. The author went to the location and tried to find the bear but to no avail. The following day there were more sightings of a small bear there. On investigating again, the author found a small female bear which appeared to be very close to dying. She could blink her eyes, but was otherwise entirely motionless. She was left alone, and was found dead in exactly the same position the following day. It turns out that she weighed only 37 pounds. She had been unable to survive the winter due to poor health and a lack of enough fat.

AVON CALLING?

At the end of July in 1987 a camper with two children came into the Porkies Headquarters and asked about bears. They had already been backpacking and had hung up their food, but a bear had damaged a pack. A sow with one cub came to his campsite and bit into a side pocket of a pack which was leaning near the tent. It seems that the camper had put foot powder, soap and suntan oil in there. It never occurred to him that bears might like the smell of such items, or consider them as food.

A backpacking youth group from Camp Amnicon experienced what was a very common occurrence in the Porkies in 1988. They lost their food to a bear. This happened at Mirror Lake on August 3rd shortly after midnight. The next morning it was discovered that the cosmetics which were apparently wisely hung with the food had not been eaten, only bitten. Perhaps the cosmetics were what attracted the bear in the first place. How essential are cosmetics while out backpacking in bear country?

In another incident, which was very similar to that described in *Raiders of the Lost Camp*, only the abandoned equipment was found after the campers deserted their camp. This incident was not reported by the campers involved. The abandoned camp was reported by other campers who discovered the camp later. Most of the equipment and supplies left behind was damaged or destroyed by a bear. The one detail about this incident which still sticks in my mind many years later concerns a bottle found at the site. What kind of bottle you ask? Was it some item essential to backpackers out there in the wilderness? A survival item? Of course not, it was a bottle of "S.E.X." brand men's cologne!

HAMMING IT UP IN PORCUPINE MOUNTAINS

Bill Perrin is a retired Porkies ranger. In April of 1992 he told me a few of his park bear tales from back in the 1960's.

On one occasion, a lady camped at the Union Bay modern campground decided to prepare an especially fine meal for her family. She purchased a fancy ham at Carlson's Supermarket in Ironwood. This was one of those with pineapple slices on it. She set out all of her goodies on the picnic table at her site including the ham, a gallon of milk, plates, utensils, etc. and called her family to come and eat.

A big bear also came. It got there before anyone got a bite of anything. And, as bears are want to do, it was a pig about the whole thing. Bears love ham. It ate every bit of the ham. While it was doing this, the campers ran for the ranger. Bill Perrin was the ranger. There wasn't really much that Bill could do. He advised the campers to be more careful with their food in the future. Meanwhile, the bear was polishing off the rest of the ham and slurping up the milk. Then, when it was all finished, it went back into the woods. The campers were hungry, and the lady of the family was furious.

BLACKBEAR DUNDEE

Bill Perrin also mentioned an incident involving a park employee he was working with one day in the Union Bay Campground. He and George Stephens went into the campground in a park pickup truck to do some work in the middle of the day. Back then, there were trash baskets at every other site along the road. As they entered the campground, two large bears were spotted towards the far end. These bears were not together, but were eating out of different trash baskets not far apart. Each of the bears was between 300 and 350 pounds. It was rather unusual to have two big bears in the campground at the same time.

George stopped the truck not far from the closer of the two bears. He got out, went to the back of the truck, and picked up a shovel out of the bed. He then nonchalantly walked over to the first bear and gave it a good swat in the butt with the flat of the shovel. It ran into the woods as did the other bear. Bill was rather stunned by George's actions. He had no idea what George had been planning to do.

Well, the bears were gone. George had scared them away, but probably not for long. They undoubtedly came right back as soon as the rangers left.

DIRTY DANCING

Back in 1979 a visitor to Porcupine Mountains reported an attempted break in of a car. The car had mud smeared all over it. It was still locked, however, and had not been entered.

What the investigating deputies found was not an attempted break in, but a bear mess. The mud on the car was from bear paw prints. The car's owner indicated he had sprayed pop on the car and had not washed it off. A bear climbed all over the car licking off the sweet residue of dried pop. (It took only sweet licks and left only footprints and scratches).

SWING HIGH, SWING LOW

The Douglas Wolk backpacking party had bear problems while camping in the Porkies. They camped at Mirror Lake near the Correction Line Trail junction. Around 10:30 P.M. on July 11, 1981, a bear showed up at camp. At that time of year it is still light enough to see. Doug indicated that they had hung their packs 18 feet above the ground, and at least 4 feet from the tree trunk.

The bear ascended the tree, jumped onto a pack, and hung there swinging until the pack tore off the frame. The bear duplicated this performance for the other pack. According to my source, one pack was totally destroyed while the other one was only ruined. I'm not quite sure what the difference is between destroyed and ruined. Perhaps in the second case there was some substantial part of the pack left, but not in the first case? The bear ate about $40.00 worth of food. This pigishness caused Doug and partner to leave three days early from their trip. They decided they were not going to camp for three more days without any food, and I cannot blame them.

And the moral of this *particular* tale? Repeat after me, "I will do a better job of hanging my food up next time, *but I will not hang it inside of my pack.*"

The campers were very upset by this little episode. They suggested that the bear be destroyed. It should be noted for the record that, over the years, many backpacking parties at the Porkies have had to cut their stays short due to the fact that the bears stole their food. If all the bears which have ever stolen campers' food were destroyed, there probably would not be any bears left. Aw, come on now, what fun would it be to go out into the wilderness to camp if there was no wildlife?

GRIN AND BEAR IT

People with pickup trucks sometimes have problems keeping their food away from bears while camping. On September 2, 1987 the Lockhardt party had a bear climb into the back of their pickup at the White Pine Extension Outpost Campground in the Porkies. It tried to get into their cooler. It also damaged a cooler from a nearby camp as well as the trash bin at the campground. It was a large and non-timid bear.

On September 13, 1991 at the Lost Creek Outpost Campground the Kane party was treated to a performance of the same general type. The bear was around 200 pounds in weight. The Kanes had stored all of their food in the back of the truck. The bear repeatedly climbed in to try and get their food. The campers repeatedly chased it away. In fact you might say it interfered with their rest and relaxation since this went on all night - from 12:00 P.M. to 6:00 A.M. And just think, they just as easily could have stayed home and watched television all night.

PLOP GOES THE BEAR

Sung to the tune of Pop Goes the Weasel:

> The bear was trying to get our food.
> The bear climbed up the tree.
> The bear took a jump into the air.
> PLOP GOES THE BEAR!

Porkies Ranger Bob Sprague provided the following story to the author. He told me of an incident that took place on the Big Carp River Trail one and a half miles west of the Lake of the Clouds

Scenic Area. It occurred in 1988, which was a beary bad year (pun intended). The campers involved were kept awake all night by a bear which kept climbing a tree in efforts to get at their food stash. It kept falling out of a tree and landing on the ground with a distinctive "plop." Apparently, the campers figured out a way to hang their food so that bears actually cannot get it.

Now, if the rangers could just find out what it was that these campers did to bear proof their food stash, then all backpackers could be informed and would be assured of keeping their food supplies away from the bears. Many, many backpacking parties have had to shorten their camping trips because bears have ripped off their food supplies. However, if other backpackers use the same methods to stash their food as the above campers, then they are either going to have to go without sleep and put up with "plopping" bears, or use earplugs at night.

THE GREAT OUTDOORS

Bob Sprague also related an incident in the Great Smoky Mountains which occurred to a relative of his. The problems were so great at some of their backpacking campground areas that chain link fences were installed around them to keep the bears out. It was at one of these that the real value of the fences was demonstrated. While at the campsite a large bear showed up outside the fence and tried to get in. The bruin's method was very straightforward: start some distance back from the fence, run towards the fence, and throw its hefty bulk against the chain link. It did this for hours.

Once again, the ingenuity of man has made the great outdoors a more wonderful, peaceful, safe, and enjoyable place to visit. Wouldn't you like to go there?

TAKING CARE OF BUSINESS

A youth group leader reported to the Lake of the Clouds entrance booth ranger that his group had lost almost all of their food to a bear at the Scott Creek area. There were nine separate food bags hung, one for each member of the group. They were very carefully located, high in a huge tree, over 40 feet off the ground, and on branches too small for a bear to climb out on. The bear got eight of the food bags, all by chewing off the entire branches which they were hung on. It took most of the night for it to do this. Fortunately for this camping party, they hung their food far from camp and at least got a good night's sleep.

CABIN FEVER

On July 22, 1988, the Johnson party reported to the Union Bay Campground Office that a bear had entered the Section 17 Cabin while they were away. It went in through a side window screen and got into their food stores. The next day the Johnson party reported that the bear returned to the cabin and walked around it. They were able to scare it away by banging pots and pans together.

The Ringwelski party reported that on July 30, 1988, a bear had clawed on the Big Carp River Cabin. The bear had also ripped a hole in an occupied tent next to the cabin. Bears were continually in the Big Carp River rivermouth area between the 28th and 31st. There was definitely NO food in the damaged tent, because the party had lost a tent to a bear two years previously in which food was involved and they had learned that lesson already (also, see the entries under *Bears, Lies, and Videotape.*)

CATCH ME IF YOU CAN

Roland Clisch, Porkies Maintenance Mechanic, provided some details concerning an incident which occurred during the construction of the old North Mirror Lake Trail Bridge. This happened in 1968. The bridge is located right below the Lake of the Clouds Scenic Overlook.

It seems that a bear was hanging around the area all summer. On many occasions it came out into view and watched the park crew while they were working. On this particular occasion, the bear grabbed the lunch pail of one of the young workers and ran off with it. Al Hanson, the Park's Carpenter, picked up an axe and gave chase.

Al must have been pretty fast because when he returned a short while later, he had the lunchbox. Al did not catch up to the bear, but the bear dropped the pail. Other than a good set of bear tooth marks in the lunchbox, the young man's lunch pail was in good shape.

WHO'S THAT KNOCKING AT MY DOOR?

The Witzgall party reported that on June 2, 1989 around 12:30 A.M. a bear began scratching at the Lake of the Clouds Cabin door. Mr. Witzgall banged on the door, and the bear then left. Prior cabin users have had similar encounters.

[I can just hear your kids when you read this story to them. "Mom, Dad, can we go stay in a Porkies cabin? Please? Pleeeeeeeeze?" I can also imagine the answer. "NO!"]

CLOSE ENCOUNTERS OF THE FURRED KIND

A CLOSE ENCOUNTER OF THE BARE KIND

A lady was sunning herself face down on the beach at the Big Carp 6 Bunk Cabin on June 18, 1988 (the beary bad year). On feeling something brush against her body, she looked up to be nose to nose with a bear. She made a noise, but it did not scare the bear away. The bear just wandered around and left after a short while.

A CLOSE ENCOUNTER OF THE SCARY KIND

A young couple, Dennis and Linda, from Milwaukee had an interesting encounter with one of the Porkies bruins on August 9, 1989. They were camped near the Government Peak shelter. While over looking at the shelter, a large bear approached their campsite and took some of their unsecured trail mix and nuts. The couple raised a ruckus by banging on the shelter walls and were able to get the bear to leave.

The campers then packed up their food and threw it up on the shelter roof for safekeeping. The shelter was vacant at the time. After about a half hour, the bear came back. The couple climbed up trees. The bear sniffed around the base of the trees, then climbed up the one that Dennis was in. The bear came up to within about four inches of his foot. Dennis and Linda started screaming when the bear got so close. The bear apparently didn't like that and left. So did the campers. They packed up and immediately departed at about 11:00 P.M.

FOOD WARS

Ted Amling from Camp Lincoln reported that on July 20, 1990, his group of boys was camped near the mouth of the Big Carp River. He heard a bear outside the tent, got out, and saw the bear dragging away one of their packs. He rushed at the bear yelling to scare it away. The bear took evasive action and accidentally rolled onto one of the group's tents with three boys inside. No one was hurt and the bear left. The persistent bear returned a short time later, and during that exciting episode it ran at Ted to scare him away. Ted did not leave, even though the bear came within five feet of him. There were no injuries in this incident.

The Camp Lincoln group was apparently storing their food inside of their packs, with the packs stacked on the ground under a tarp, *which is not a good idea.*

HEAVY

Roland Clisch also mentioned another incident which is out of the ordinary. Some years ago there was a problem bear at the Union Bay modern campground in the Porkies. Apparently this bear was hyperactive and could not be trapped. So, an attempt was made to tranquilize it.

The bear was shot with the tranquilizer on the east end of the campground. It panicked and ran out the campground entrance road all the way to the junction with highway M-107. At that time there was a very large tree right on the corner of the entrance. This bear rushed up the tree. It climbed up to the very top of the tallest branch and tried to climb even higher. It fell out of the tree and died instantly upon hitting the ground.

Whether it fell due to slipping, being drugged, or due to some other factor is not known for sure. However, the description of the incident makes it sound like the bear was actually trying to climb higher where there was no more tree.

MR. BLACKBEAR'S NEIGHBORHOOD

On the night of May 16th, 1992, a backpacking group in Porcupine Mountains had a bad experience. The group consisted of fourteen youngsters and leaders. They had planned to stay at the Big Carp 4

Bunk and Big Carp 6 Bunk Cabins in the Park. There was some kind of mixup, and so the group only had use of the 4 Bunk Cabin.

That night was one of those rainy, windy, miserable ones that you hope never to experience while on vacation. The leaders decided to put all fourteen people into the cabin, and to put all 14 of the packs outside under a tarp.

They all got a very good night's sleep in spite of the crowding. There were no annoying disturbances which the group members were aware of to interfere with their sleep. In the morning a terrible discovery was made. All of their food was gone! All of the packs had been damaged by a bear (or bears) during the night. A couple of packs were missing. Those were found over a hundred yards away, where the bear had dragged them. Some of the packs were completely demolished, even the frames having been chewed on! There were also fresh claw marks on the side of the cabin where the packs had been stacked.

The bear which ate all that freeze dried food probably spent the entire next day drinking water. Also, he (or she) will probably hang around the Big Carp River / Lake Superior area all summer. 1992 is definitely shaping up to be another beary bad year.

EVEN PEOPLE WHO ARE BEARANOID MIGHT HAVE A BEAR ATTACK

How dangerous are black bears generally? Well, considering the very large numbers of backpackers who camp in the Porkies every summer (not to mention all the other parks in the country where black bears abound), it is obvious that the bears are not going out of their way to harm people. Bears are clearly potentially dangerous, but they are not hunting down campers for food, nor are they indiscriminately injuring hikers for the fun of it. This is not to say that there are no cases where bears have injured or killed people. There are such cases, but they are rare.

There have been two bear caused injury cases from Porcupine Mountains Wilderness State Park, one fatality, and one probable case of a bear biting someone inside a tent. All of these incidents were described earlier in this book. As for cases of black bears stalking humans for food, they are exceedingly rare, and the author is not aware of any such incidents in the western Upper Peninsula of Michigan. Here is a listing of every such stalking incident that the author is aware of, where and approximately when it occurred. All of these incidents are listed from memory, and for reference only:

Around 1959 near Brimley, Michigan a bear (around 150 lbs.) killed and ate a five year old girl. It grabbed the girl, who was playing with an older girl, in broad daylight and carried her into the woods. This occurred near a forest fire watch tower where her father worked. The bear was later located and killed, and confirmation was made that it was the bear involved and that it had eaten the child.

In 1977 a bear in Ontario killed and partially buried three sixteen year old boys. The partial burying indicates the bear was after food and intended to eat them.

In the late 1970's a U.S. Geological Survey worker in Alaska was stalked and attacked by a large black bear. The worker survived, but lost her forearms. An account of the incident was published in one of the major women's monthly magazines (*Redbook*, I think).

In the early 1980's a black bear (around 250 lbs.) in Minnesota grabbed a 12 year old boy in his yard and dragged him into the woods. His father was able to get a rifle and kill the bear. The boy survived; his scalp had been torn off by the bear and was reattached.

In 1987 a bear of around 200 pounds in weight attacked people on two different occasions in the Boundary Waters Canoe Area of Minnesota. In the first case a camper named Tyson Crowder (19 years old) from Marysville, Tennessee was attacked on Monday, September 14th in the evening. He managed to get away from the bear, but was injured. He had numerous puncture wounds and lacerations including a 6" cut on the right side of his scalp where he was bitten. He also had a broken shoulder blade.

The following day the same bear attacked S. Jeremy Cleveland (age 52) from Minnetonka, Minnesota who was preparing to leave his camp around 1 P.M. with his 29 year old son, James. When the bear appeared and silently approached, the two Clevelands ran into the lake, but the bear caught the older Cleveland in the water and bit him around the head and neck. The younger Cleveland dragged his father, with the bear clinging to him, onto the shore and hit the bear in the head with a paddle. Another hit with the paddle on the neck caused the bear to release his father and back up. The men quickly got in their canoe and paddled away. Jeremy Cleveland had a total of 19 bite marks with 13 being on the neck.

The information on the above incident is condensed from the September 17, 1987 Duluth Times-Herald. That article also gave numerous bits of information from two persons with extensive experience in dealing with bears: Lynn Rogers of the U.S. Forest Service and Dave Garshelis of the Minnesota D.N.R. They indicated that they had never had to deal with a bear which was clearly trying to attack humans as a food source in the combined 27 years of their service. Mr. Garshelis indicated that there have been 23 documented cases of black bears attacking humans since 1900.

Undoubtedly there are other such incidents, however, as stated before, they are the exception rather than the rule. There are, of course, other types of incidents where people were injured by bears, but the bears were not trying to eat the people. One such story in this book involved a hunter who shot a cub bear and its mother. Another involved a backpacker who was exceedingly careless with his food supplies.

Now that everyone is considering cancelling their future camping trips, it is time to try to put this more gory information in perspective. Over the past 47 years at Porcupine Mountains Wilderness State Park there has been one human fatality involving a black bear. The bear did not attempt to eat the person (for the story, see *She Was the Terror of the Porkies*). The person died from internal injuries received from falling out of a tree during a bear incident.

There were two injuries of campers during that 47 year period. In the earlier case the parent of a small child was attempting to put the child on the back of what was a problem bear in order to get a picture at the Carp Lake Mine picnic area along M-107. This occurred in the 1960s. The child was scratched by the bear (no major injuries), and the bear was destroyed. In the second case the careless backpacker received numerous bites and lacerations and required many stitches (for details of this incident, see *All the Wrong Moves*).

However, no one can be **guaranteed** safety from wild animals. Everyone has to take some precautions when in the woods, and pay some attention to what is going on around them. The following story will bear this out.

AGAINST ALL ODDS

Ms. Margaret Furlong DeChant of Newberry, Michigan brought the following story to the attention of the author. It concerns an incident which happened to her father, Mr. F. P. (Pat) Furlong, who was a District Supervisor for the Michigan Conservation Department at the time. This incident occurred in mid July sometime prior to 1946.

Pat had been walking around the woods in southeast Luce County. He crossed an opening of about six acres in the poplar forest. Near the edge of the opening he saw a large bear which moved off into the underbrush. Mr. Furlong was very used to seeing bears in the woods and thought nothing of it - that is, until a short while later when he heard a noise and looked up on a slight bank nearby to see the bear watching him. Instead of leaving, the bear came down off the bank towards Pat and stopped about 15 feet away.

Now the bear definitely had Pat's full attention! It took two steps towards Pat. He tried to scare the bruin by shouting at it and holding up a map. It was not frightened by the shouting or the map as it took a couple more steps towards him. Pat started to slowly back away from the bear and he threw the map into its face. The bear slowly advanced, walking right over the map.

Pat now panicked. He turned and ran. The bear followed, slowly at first, and then picking up speed. Pat could hear it coming behind him. Pat started thinking while running. He knew he could never outrun a bear. He forced himself to turn and face his antagonist. At the same time, Pat reconnoitered the clearing he was in. He wanted to climb a tree, but the only nearby ones were small poplars. So, he continued backing away from the bear towards a large spruce tree near the middle of the clearing.

The bear stopped when Pat turned to face it, but it started to pursue Pat again as he backed away. Pat was forced to start throwing things at the bear because it was getting so close. He threw pieces of rotting wood from stumps, chunks of bark, sticks, and handfuls of sand. The bear would stop for a second or two while Pat was sending a constant stream of debris into its face, but Pat had to hop from spot to spot in order to maintain a good supply of throwables.

Pat backed into an old building location where he grabbed two short pieces of board. Instead of throwing these at the bruin, he struck them together. This noise stopped the bear. Pat continued hitting the two pieces of board together and stepped toward the bear. It backed up. Pat went on the offensive, whacking the boards together only a few feet away from the bears' nose. Finally, the bear turned and slowly headed for the woods with Pat right behind making as much noise as he could with the small pieces of wood. Pat threw the boards at the woods as the bear entered them. This was a **BIG** mistake.

The bear went into the woods only about forty feet, turned around, and came back towards Pat. All of the above described actions were repeated over again in the same order. Pat turned and ran from the bear. He heard it start out after him right away. As the bear picked up speed and closed in on Pat, he swung around to face the bear. Pat once again had to back away slowly while throwing things into the bear's face. The bear paused now and then when the barrage was heaviest, then it would press in on Pat. Pat tried pulling up small trees by the roots and hitting the bear over the head with them, but to no avail.

Pat thought of things he could do which might stop the bear. He decided to attempt lighting some grass on fire. As soon as he tried, the bear came closer due to the slacking off on throwing things at it. Pat happened upon an old dishpan which he hit with a stick. This stopped the bear. Once again, the occurrences above were all repeated. Pat pounded on the pan as hard as he could and "chased" the bear back to the edge of the woods. This time, however, he did not throw away his noisemaker.

Pat decided to stay near the edge of the clearing and attempt to keep the bear in the woods. The bear stopped about thirty feet into the trees. Pat walked along thirty feet from the edge of the clearing pounding on his dishpan and pausing to throw suitable pieces of wood into the trees when he encountered them along the way. The bear followed along staying about thirty feet into the woods. Around they went for awhile as the shadows of the trees got longer. Finally, Pat threw a chunk of wood into the trees, but the bear was gone. Pat checked around and could not see it anywhere.

Then, Pat walked very quickly out of the area and back to his car, which was about a half mile away.

MYSTERY, HE WROTE

The following two incidents are included in this revision of True Bear Tales because bears were involved at some time during the incidents. They involve the discovery in Porcupine Mountains Wilderness State Park of a human body in one case, and of body parts in the other. In the first case enough information was available to determine that death was not caused by a bear. However, at the time the body was discovered, it was assumed that a bear attack had probably occurred. In the second case, no determination of cause of death was ever made. It remains a true mystery to this day, and no one knows to what extent bears may have been involved in the death, if at all.

FEAR NO EVIL

On Tuesday July 27, 1982, Mike Rafferty and George Cameron, two off duty rangers from Porcupine Mountains Wilderness State Park were hiking on the Escarpment Trail in the park. They stopped to rest on Cloud Peak. While there, they noticed a very foul smell. After looking around for its source, they found a carry bag and started finding various pieces of clothing. As they discovered more pieces of clothing, the smell grew even worse. When they discovered a pair of boots, they both knew it was not just a dead animal they were going to find. Eventually they located the source of the smell - a decomposing human body. Immediately they went to the park headquarters and reported their discovery.

The Sheriff and several deputies, the Coroner, the Park Manager, Mike, and George all went to the site. It was sort of assumed by the law enforcement officers that an animal, probably a bear, was involved in the death. The body had been partially eaten. Also, it had been dragged to its current location by an animal or animals. For this reason, the deputies all went armed with long guns.

Mike Rafferty had seen the man whose body he found about two weeks earlier. He recognized the carry bag found at the site, not the body. Mike had given him, a black man in his late forties from Detroit, a ride up to the Lake of the Clouds Scenic Area. That or the following evening, Dan Urbanski, a photographer, had met Mike at Paul's bar in Silver City. Dan mentioned seeing a lone black man on Cloud Peak because it was sort of unusual and the man had no camping gear. Dan indicated the man seemed very tired.

What later investigation turned up proved beyond doubt that a bear was not involved in the death. The man, whose first name was William, was a very religious person. William believed it was necessary to fast for 40 days in order for his soul to be saved. He had actually attempted this several times down in Detroit, but his friends and relatives always saved him. I say saved him because William was diabetic. If he did not eat regularly, he would go into a coma and die.

Thus, William had purposefully come all the way to Porcupine Mountains Wilderness State Park in order to be able to complete a 40 day fast without interruption. He probably died his first night on the trail at Cloud Peak. While a bear probably ate part of his body later and dragged it away from its original resting place, a bear was not the cause of William's death.

This mystery was solved. The next one was not.

BLACK MOON RISING

Late on Sunday November 19, 1968, a deer hunter near Buckshot Cabin in the Porkies made a gruesome discovery. He was hunting in two inches of new snow about one mile east of the cabin and two hundred yards from the Lake Superior shoreline. He saw what looked like a boot laying on its side with a long branch sticking out of it. On investigating he found that it was a boot laying on its side, but it was not a long branch sticking out of it. It was a human leg bone still attached to a foot inside of the boot.

The hunter was shaken. He blazed a trail to the lakeshore and marked the location. Then he went to report what he had seen. A search of the immediate area was made the following day by Ontonagaon County Sheriff Powelson, Deputy Shankle, Park Manager Balbough, Ranger Poulos, Conservation Officer Haltug, and State Trooper Carey. They turned up the mate to the boot about fifty feet away from the first one, and several pieces of bone which had been chewed on. The boot, which was still laced with the foot inside, had deep teeth marks in the inseam and sole. The other boot had chew marks on the heel. The bite marks appear to have been those of a bear.

Unlike the first mystery above which was later solved as far as who the body was and the cause of death, no such determinations were ever made for this case. A bear was almost assuredly involved in eating part of the body, but was it involved in the death? Nobody knows.

ABOUT THE AUTHOR

David E. Young is in his eighteenth year as a park ranger at Porcupine Mountains Wilderness State Park, and has also worked at Fort Wilkins State Park near Copper Harbor, Michigan. He began working for the Michigan Department of Natural Resources (Parks Division) during the summers while attending Michigan State University.

Since 1981, Dave has done weekly collection and testing of acidity in rain and snow samples for contractors to the U.S. Environmental Protection Agency. Also, for the past twelve years, Dave has been a chief steward for the Michigan State Employees Association.

In late 1991, Dave published a documentary history of the U. S. Bill of Rights with special emphasis on the intent of the Second Amendment (right to keep and bear arms). Having diligently researched the subject for over twenty years, Dave did all typing, editing and also typesetting of the 876 page volume himself, just as he did for *True Bear Tales*.

Collecting Lake Superior Agate specimens is Dave's favorite hobby. He also enjoys sea kayaking on Lake Superior.

Dave lives in Ontonagon, Michigan with his wife, Arlene, and their four children, Jon, Amy, David, and Tom.

ALSO AVAILABLE FROM GOLDEN OAK BOOKS

The ORIGIN of the SECOND AMENDMENT; A Documentary History in Commentaries on Liberty, Free Government and an Armed Populace during the formation of the Bill of Rights
Edited by David E. Young.

This volume is a collection of documents consisting of our ancestors' opinions from the period when the U.S. Constitution was written concerning its defects and the need to amend it with a Bill of Rights. It also contains every available document relating to the interpretation of the Second Amendment from that period (1787-1792).

Library Binding — 876 Pages — 6x9 Size — Acid Free Paper
$50.00 per copy plus $5.00 shipping and handling.
(Michigan residents please add 4% state sales tax.)
Discounts are not available for this volume.
All orders should be sent directly to:
GOLDEN OAK BOOKS
(See copyright page for address.)

PART III

The Third Edition Update

1992 To 1995

PART III CONTENTS

PART THREE

THE THIRD EDITION UPDATE

1992 To 1995

1992

A BEARY BAD YEAR

THE BEARS WENT OVER THE MOUNTAINS

1992 was an unusual year for black bear activity. It started as a fairly cool year weather wise. On approximately the first day of summer, there was a hard frost throughout the western Upper Peninsula which undoubtedly destroyed a large portion of the bear population's future natural food supply. This resulted in many of the bears heading directly to the nearest towns for sources of food. Since there are no more open dumps, the next best thing for the bears is the garbage dumpsters in which restaurants, grocery stores and other commercial enterprises dispose of their trash.

In addition to the bears in the towns, there were some bad, bold bears in the interior of Porcupine Mountains Wilderness State Park. Their activities were reported at the Carp Rivermouths, Shining Cloud Falls, the Correction Line Shelter, and especially at Mirror Lake. There was plenty of food being carried around by backpackers to keep these bears fed without them having to leave for town.

By late summer, there was adequate natural food for the bear population. The bears, however, were already well set at getting their food either in and around the towns or from the backpackers in the Porkies. The late summer berry crops did not attract the bears from the towns, nor did they divert the backpack raiding bears from their nefarious ways.

THE LOWDOWN ON THE UPDATE

The bear problems were so numerous and bad in the towns of the western Upper Peninsula during this summer that bear stories were continually in the newspapers. The following collection consists entirely of newspaper headlines, story titles, editorial headings and section headings. They are taken from the Ontonagon Herald (O), the Ironwood Globe (I), and the Houghton Daily Mining Gazette (H). These titles, many of which were intended as updates on the continuing bear problems, will give the reader a fairly good general idea of what was going on in the towns located within bear country in 1992.

July 7 (H) BEWARE: BEARS RUNNING AMUCK IN HOUGHTON

July 7 (I) Foraging bear complaints from Silver City area

July 8 (H) Beware of Bear

July 10 (I) Bearable? - Bruins Entertain

July 15 (O) Beware of Bear

July 24 (I) Beary Interesting

July 30 (I) Ironwood Bear Menace Continues

July 31 (I) Bear Precautions Wise, says WDNR

August 12 (I) Bear Update No.???

August 14 (I) Bear Update . . .

August 17 (H) Bear Complaints on the Increase

August 20 (H) Beware of Bear! - Warning: Bears on the Loose - Bear Alert

August 20 (I) Bold - Hungry Critters - At the Porkies

August 22 (O) Car / Bear Accident

August 24 (H) Beware of Bear

August 25 (I) Bear Visits Boss - Bear Total Rising

August 26 (I) Bear Still Active

August 27 (I) Urban Wildlife - Hunger Makes Bruins Unbearable

August 29 (H) Berry pickers reminded to watch out for bears

September 1 (I) Bear Relief

September 8 (I) Rummy Bear

September 9 (I) Bears: Amusing, Dangerous Creatures Northwoods Favorites - Surprise!

September 15 (H) Man Kills Bear

September 23 (I) Bears: Humankind Stand in Awe

Is everyone getting the picture here? The author does not recall any previous, or subsequent year for that matter, which produced such a bumper crop of local newspaper stories regarding problems with the tourists' favorite animal, the black bear.

THE SUMMER OF '92

There were some early bear problems in 1992. See pages 77-78 and 100 for some early incidents that year. As stated above, the early summer frost reduced the normal midsummer food supplies of the bears. By July, the trend for bear problems in 1992 became clearly evident. Many bears had abandoned the forest and gone to town. They congregated near places where there were garbage dumpsters, such as restaurants and food stores with deli's.

Silver City, being so close to the Porcupine Mountains, had its fair share of summer bears. One person bicycling around town on the warm summer evening of July 13th counted eight different bears at various locations in town. Also, the Tunstall's, who operate the Silver City General Store, were treated to a morning bear fight behind their house to start off that same day.

There was one especially large and notable bear which hung around the Silver City area for a couple of years. Everyone referred to him as Oscar. Oscar was estimated to weigh around 450 pounds - he was a big boy. Oscar was easily recognized not only by his massive size, but also by a very noticeable white patch on his chest. He was a regular evening visitor at the End of the Rainbow Restaurant. Oscar also visited the other garbage dumpsters in the area.

There were some attempts to discourage the bears at various dumpster locations with varying degrees of success. The Best Western Porcupine Mountains Lodge placed electric fence wire all around the top edge and sides of their wooden enclosure containing their dumpster. The bears defeated this initially by digging under the edges. Placement of additional wire right around the base solved the problem. The Porcupine Mountains Lodge was probably the only success story though.

An electric wire barrier was attempted around the dumpster at the End of the Rainbow. It was successful at chasing away bears the first time they came into contact with it, but the bears did not leave the area. They hung around until the power was off or some other bear damaged the wire, thus making passage to the dumpster possible. The fence was later taken down and the evening bear show went on as usual.

A typical evening at the End of the Rainbow would include several different bears coming out of the surrounding woods to grab a bag or piece of garbage and carry it into the woods for processing. The dumpster was located directly ahead of the main parking area. Tourists, both campers and motelers, would show up an hour or so before sunset and hang around having ice cream cones or whatever while waiting for the bears to show up. This human behavior encouraged the restaurant operators to tolerate the bears and be willing to clean up the horrific mess every morning.

Eventually, a bear would wander out from the woods and get into the dumpster. Oscar developed the habit of getting into the dumpster by tipping it over on its side. He had no trouble whatsoever doing this. Meanwhile, the tourists were ooooing and ahhhhing, taking pictures, pointing, and generally running around back at the cars trying to get a better vantage point. The people who brought their motor homes and climbed on top to watch and videotape had the very best view.

Up in the Copper Harbor area, the same trend was occurring. There had already been a territorial squabble between two large bears right in front of the Copper Goose Gift Shop in town. Karl and Pat Kazeks, the shop's proprietors, were in their Suburban in front of the shop when this occurred. The bears bumped into their vehicle several times during their tussle. When large bears rumble, things do tend to shake and tumble.

The Kazeks also told the author about another bear - a really big one - which tended to hang around the Harbor Haus Restaurant. It had a regular nap every day between 2:30 and 4:30 in the afternoon. This was spent lying in the cool shade in a ditch just down the street from the restaurant, while all of the restaurant's patrons were driving right by it completely unaware that it was there.

Then there were the problems of the new proprietors of the Country Lane Bakery and Gifts Shop in Copper Harbor. Bonnie Harrer and family were from Illinois. Bonnie indicated that they were not really used to having bears come onto their porch to steal food out of a refrigerator or climb on the roof of their house just because they were having pizza. This bear activity was all new to them, but they remembered to get out their camera when the bear was around. They got a really good picture of the bear on their roof too.

Later in July, I stopped at the Fort Wilkins State Park office. Bob Hill, Assistant Park Manager, who has received several honorary awards from the community for his bear live trapping and relocating efforts in the past, had been at it again. He showed me the back of his brown Suburban, which was covered with little blue spots - billberry slosh from the bears spitting it out of the livetrap he trailered behind his vehicle. I also noticed that a bear trap was set right behind the Park's office.

Meanwhile, back near the Porkies, there were bears fighting in the woods behind Ranger Jim Richardson's house in White Pine. I imagine there were lots of territorial disputes that summer. With a large portion of the available food concentrated near towns, and towns not being the bears' normal territory, territorial disputes were inevitable.

JOE'S BEAR AND GRILL

This story was widely publicized in the surrounding region shortly after it occurred on July 19, 1992. It is another of those out of the ordinary bear happenings which remind us that bears should always be considered as quite unpredictable.

Summer Ranger Joe Jacobson was manning the Presque Isle Campground Office at the west end of Porcupine Mountains State Park. That evening around 6:45 PM was a slow period of time. The only people who had been by the office lately were some children who were playing.

A black bear approached the building, stood up at the public contact window and pounded its forepaws on the window. This bear had been around the area lately getting into the garbage. Joe figured he would scare the bear away by pounding back, but the bear did not pay any attention to what Joe was doing. It went around the office, window by window, pounding its forepaws on them. This went on for about fifteen minutes. Then the bear apparently tired of trying to frighten Joe and left.

Joe then went outside only to discover that the bear had climbed into the back of the park pickup truck next to the office. Joe now thought he could really scare the bear by banging his hands loudly against the hood of the truck and yelling at the bear simultaneously. Unfortunately, Joe was wrong. This did not frighten the bear, but apparently made the bear angry.

The bear came right out of the truck and went towards Joe. Joe was somewhat surprised and fled into the office to escape, now having realized that this was not your average bear. The bear followed Joe to the door and repeated the banging with forepaws there. Some campers had arrived at about this time and were videotaping this from their vehicles. After a few minutes the bear left. It did not seem to like Joe very much at all.

About an hour later, campers reported that the bear was tearing apart the wooden trash storage bin located just outside of the Presque Isle Campground. Joe went there and noticed that three boards were torn from the structure and garbage was strewn around the area. The bear was off to the side a short distance watching Joe as he cleaned up the area. Joe attempted several times to scare the bear by yelling at it, stomping his feet and blowing the truck horn. None of this had any affect upon the bear.

Joe had to leave for a couple minutes and when he returned the bear was back inside the trash storage bin. At about 8:45 PM, a camper carrying a bag of garbage to the bin had to drop it and run because the bear left the bin and went towards him to get the garbage. The camper apparently did not want to meet the bear that much.

Joe tried to frighten the bear again, but it did not work. This bear was a lot like Presque Isle's Boo Boo from back in 1985. Since this one clearly was not your average bear, let's call him Yogi. Yogi had seen everything tried in attempts to scare him away, and so he was not frightened by anything. Besides, this was not a game to Yogi, this was a food gathering situation and thus he was not to be trifled with by mere campers and rangers. Yogi nipped the garbage bag dropped by the camper, who had decided not to meet him, and trotted off into the woods near the garbage bin to tear it apart.

During the next two hours, Yogi raided the bin at least seven times. Twice he wandered away into the campground to snitch two different coolers and a couple pounds of hamburger despite serious attempts to drive him away. When Joe left the campground around 11:00 PM, Yogi was back inside of the garbage bin. Yes sir, all indications were that Yogi was destined to be another Boo Boo.

Well, not quite. Yogi knew nothing of Boo Boo's fate, or he might have mended his ways. The rangers knew what mistake they had made with Boo Boo, and they were not about to make it again. This time, if they trapped a super problem bear, they did not plan to release it anywhere near the Park. Boo Boo had been trapped and released within the Park on four occasions.

Yogi returned to the Campground Office the next day and repeated his actions of the previous day. He left the area just a few minutes before Ranger Rick Tessmer arrived with a bear trap, which was promptly set up near one of Yogi's paths to the destroyed garbage bin. Within less than one half hour, Yogi ended up in the trap and was then given an all expenses paid trip by the State of Michigan to another location far, far away from the Porkies. He would undoubtedly have been another Boo Boo if the rangers had committed another boo boo by trapping and releasing him four times in the Park.

Yogi's departure allowed Joe to finally pick up all the strewn garbage and repair the bin with some assurance that it was not going to be entirely for naught. Also, Joe had a lot more time to ponder why Yogi seemed to dislike him so much. He remembered that the day Yogi first banged on the windows, some children had been playing around the campground office shortly before Yogi showed up. The kids had tried to annoy Joe, but he had ignored them. A couple minutes later when he heard them make another noise, he had quickly closed the sliding glass window used for public contact.

It was then that Yogi stood up outside the window and started to bang away at it. Perhaps, just perhaps, Yogi had his snout or paw near the window and got pinched? This might account for Yogi's fairly unusual display of behavior and apparent anger towards Joe. We will never know for sure, but it is something to wonder about.

A BEARNAPPING

The Woodson YMCA group out of Wausau had an interesting encounter. They got a much better than average look at a yearling bear. It came into their camp at the Big Carp Rivermouth area. The rangers call this Carptown due to the three park cabins and all the backpackers who congregate around there. This incident occurred on July 22nd.

The bear grabbed one of the group's packs. It just happened to be the one pack with a candy bar inside of it! What do you think, was that bear lucky or what? The bruin was not afraid of the campers at all and could not be scared away. It hung around the camp area for about a half hour, then laid down in the middle of camp and took a half hour nap. Eating candy bars is tiring work for a bear you know.

TERMINAL VELOCITY

Rick Tessmer is a Porkies Ranger who has an unending sense of humor. His bear report of July 24th, 1992 is not your typical guy had a problem with a bear and lost his food and some gear report. No, Rick knows how to add pizzaz to the description of a bear encounter so that the readers get the message and do not doze off.

Brent Johnson had a bear encounter while trout fishing near Lake of the Clouds in the Porkies and reported it to Ranger Rick. Rick described the encounter as if it were some kind of race. Brent noticed that he was being followed by a bear. He was not overly happy about this, so he speeded up his walking somewhat. Every time he decided to go faster, so did the bear. According to Rick, Brent finally accelerated to what he hoped to be "escape velocity" and maintained this extremely fast speed for about a half hour. The bear supposedly lost interest in Brent, and Brent lost the bear.

While at escape velocity, Brent had taken some evasive action. He had cooled himself as well as lightened his load by getting rid of a considerable list of items. These including a red flannel shirt, a black bag containing his waders, a handful of bagels, and the two brook trout he had caught and was taking home.

Rick would have us believe that the bear lost interest in Brent, but we all know it never had any interest in Brent in the first place. Since it probably didn't need a flannel shirt or a pair of waders, it must have really been after either the bagels or those tasty brook trout, which it could easily smell. I bet black bears especially like brook trout, and this one got bagels to boot (no pun intended here!)

Rick's final comment on his report was, "Bear approached to within 20-25 feet before Mr. Johnson accelerated to terminal velocity."

THE BEAR MALL

Those hungry Porkies bears which did go to town in 1992 had a couple of places to pick from. They could go due east to Silver City or southeast to White Pine. There are a couple of restaurants at the White Pine Mall, Antonio's and the Konteka. The Konteka ended up being a major bear target. The local Conservation Officer, Jackie Strauch, trapped at least four bears there that summer.

The Konteka, in addition to having bowling lanes and a bar, has large picture windows looking out towards the woods. Friday night there is always a much frequented seafood buffet. I believe it was during a Friday buffet that one of the several bears hanging around the area went up to the windows, stood up with paws on the glass watching everyone inside eating, and shook the windows a few times. Just think, if he had really tried harder, he might have been able to go in and have all the seafood he wanted.

While the Konteka's customers were used to seeing the bears outside, they definitely were not used to having them behave like this one did. Undoubtedly this particular bear was one of those which Jackie Strauch had to trap and haul away.

KICKING OUT THE JAMBS

Regarding bears, which Jackie Strauch trapped that year, I remember one instance in particular which she told me about. She had captured a large boar in the Ironwood area and was hauling it away to the east along U.S. 2. As she drove along down the highway, her vehicle seemed to jerk or hesitate regularly. She looked into her rearview mirror to see if the bear in the trap was behaving. Whatever it was doing, it was not standing upright.

Instead, the very unhappy bruin had rolled over on his back in the trap and was proceeding to kick the trap's door with both rear legs at regular intervals. This tremendous amount of force being applied to the trap door was actually noticeably slowing down the vehicle slightly. Upon inspection, after the bear was released, Jackie noticed that many of the welds on the jambs or channels which the sliding door fits inside of were broken.

When the author arrived at the Porkies Service Area for work the following day, the trap was parked right in front of the repair garage with the door laying on the ground next to it. This was to make sure Jim Rogan or Jerry Monk, the Park's Auto Mechanics, would notice and repair it right away. There were so many bear complaints and problems that summer in the towns that Jackie wanted to avoid any unnecessary down time for the trap.

THE GREAT OUTDOORS II

Imagine having the opportunity to visit the beautiful Porcupine Mountains Wilderness State Park and Mirror Lake, Michigan's highest lake nestled in the Park's peaks. Many Park visitors have gone to visit this wonderful area which is dotted with huge rock outcroppings and completely carpeted with virgin timber. The Lepisto family from Racine, Wisconsin decided to take the hike to the middle of the Porkies on August 6th of 1992.

Four members of the family went for the hike, parents Gene and Sandra, plus two of their sons, Brad and Ryan aged 19 and 11 respectively. They hiked to Mirror Lake on the north route from Lake of the Clouds. As they got to within about one mile of their goal, they noticed bear droppings along the side of the North Mirror Lake Trail. Shortly after this, they met a family which was staying at one of the Mirror Lake cabins. The subject of bears came up and the cabin users told the Lepisto's that they had cooked some fish outdoors at their cabin hoping to eat it outside. Unfortunately, a bear came along and rangers had advised them to go indoors.

The Lepisto's continued on their way. As they reached Mirror Lake, Sandra noticed a black bear about 30 feet away in the brush. Shortly after she noticed the bear, it rustled around in the underbrush and Brad noticed it. It then stood up on its hind legs to look at them. In this position, the bear looked quite threatening. The Mirror Lake 8 Bunk Cabin was directly ahead of the Lepistos and just within sight, so they all began to run for shelter there.

The bear followed them towards the cabin. As the Lepisto's rushed up with relief to open the cabin door, they had a terrible shock. The door was locked! They sped around the corner of the cabin seriously considering climbing up on the cabin roof. Then they spotted the pit toilet out behind the cabin. They all hurried into the outhouse. It was decided to leave the door open for now since they did not know exactly where the bear was located. It did not show up right away and may have headed to the south they hoped. Since it was not then in sight, they started out with intentions of going directly back to the north - pronto.

After going only about 50 feet from the outhouse, Brad spotted the bear coming toward them and only a very short distance away. He turned, yelling and pushing, causing everyone to panic and tumultuously rush back to the outhouse. In the process, Brad knocked down Ryan, then picked him up and literally threw him into the little building.

Once inside the safety of the outhouse, Brad locked the door and braced to keep it closed. The others stood up on the seat area and looked out the screened louvers to see where the bear was and what it was up to. Sure enough, this time it was right outside. The thoroughly frightened family discussed what to do. They reasoned that the bear was after food, not after them. This self assurance did not abate their fears any, however. The bear was lumbering around the cabin at this time.

After going around the cabin, the bear started back towards the outhouse again. Gene pounded on the wall and shouted. This had no visible effect upon the bear. The bear wandered around the area within sight for about twenty minutes, then wandered away out of sight. The Lepisto's decided to cut their Mirror Lake stay very short. They split.

As they hurried off, Brad tossed away the health cakes and oranges which they had brought along to snack on. Brad ripped the cakes and oranges apart before tossing them so the bear would be more likely to smell them and go for them rather than follow the Lepistos. Afterward, the family was sorry they had thrown their food to leave for the bear. They realized that it was the very type of activity which caused bears to behave the way this one had.

Now that they were flying down the trail unimpeded, the fact that Brad's hands were all covered with orange smell started to bother them. They feared that if the bear liked the oranges, it might follow Brad to the ends of the earth. So Brad, not slowing down for a moment, sprayed a generous amount of insect repellent onto his hands while running north along the trail.

Well, so much for the idyllic trip to the most beautiful part of Michigan. Campers and hikers everywhere often have a much different experience in their outings than what they planned to have before setting out into the wilds. The Lepisto's adventure was definitely one to fit into this category with a vengeance. They had not even remembered to get out their camera, brought to take pictures of the beautiful surroundings, to take a picture of their tormentor. They indicated that one bear encounter is exactly one too many.

There was also another incident on August 6th in the Porkies. It involved Boy Scout Troop 31 who were backpacking in the Park. The group was harassed all night by a bear which attempted unsuccessfully to get their food cache. The bear was very bold, approaching so closely to the campers that this alone caused them great concern. The bear involved was very much used to people, and sounds very much like it might have been the very same bear which the Lepistos ran into a little earlier in the day.

THE CANDYMAN

On the 11th of August, some backpackers lost a pack and a tent to a bear while the campers watched. This bear incident occurred about a mile west of the Big Carp River Shelter.

On the 13th, at about 9:00 PM, a bold bear visited a camp at Mirror Lake. It got into their food, some of which was hung up and some of which was not for some reason. The bear ripped a pack, circled around the tent, and so thoroughly unnerved the campers that they soon abandoned their camp and started to hike out towards Lake of the Clouds. The bear followed the campers, who had fed the bear candy bars. Do not feed bears candy bars.

The following day there was almost an exact repeat of the above incident with a different camp. This time the bear was able to get their food sacks from the tree. It was impossible to scare the bruin away. The campers cut short their stay and hiked out to the north. The bear followed them for the full four miles. Whenever the campers stopped along the way, the bear stopped. What fun, eh?

STICKS AND STONES CAN BREAK MY BONES, BUT FIRE IS NO BIG DEAL

Two days later on the 16th at the Correction Line Shelter area, a very persistent bear entered the camp of the Manness party who were preparing their dinner. They had planned to stop and eat and then hike another two miles afterwards to avoid possible bear problems. The bear, which was large and unafraid, grabbed some of their food and took off with it. It returned a bit later and grabbed a pack, but dropped the pack after the campers pelted it with sticks and yelled. The bear would not leave, however, and sat chewing on the campers' loaf of bread.

The campers prepared some sticks with white gas soaked rags on the ends and thrust them in the bear's face as it sat and ate. The bear was exceedingly unconcerned about the burning sticks being brandished near it, contrary to what the campers apparently expected. The campers next packed up quickly and fled down the trail. The bear followed them for a mile.

When the group thought they had really lost the bear, they set up camp and hung their remaining food. Later that night the bear caught up with them, got their cache out of the tree, and ate all of their remaining food. This undoubtedly caused them to be hungry and leave the Park early. Can you imagine going on vacation hiking and having to fast at the same time?

FOREST GRUMP

A large bear was getting into garbage cans at the Porkies Organization Campground and trash dumpsters at the Silver Sands Motel and the Union River Campground. This bear was also fairly bold, so everyone was happy when it was finally trapped on August 18th.

Jerry Monk from the Porkies was assigned to haul it far, far away down to National Forest Highway 16. While driving down that road, Jerry must have hit some really tremendous bumps, because the trap rolled over after coming unhooked from the truck. The only things left connecting the truck and trap together were the safety chains. Fortunately, there were some people who helped Jerry right the trap and get it hooked back up to his vehicle. This was a brand new Chevy pickup, which now had a sizeable dent in the brand new tailgate. I don't think Jerry got to haul any bears away after this one.

The bear did not seem to be any worse for the wear. Jerry said that while the bruin seemed to be calm when he released it, the bear was also obviously miffed. It came out of the trap very slowly and turned to look at Jerry for awhile. Then it walked a short distance away and paused to turn and look at Jerry again. Then it walked a little further and looked back at Jerry a third time. Jerry said he could just imagine the bear thinking something like, "Where did you ever learn to drive?"

THIS BEAR'S FOR YOU

Summer Ranger Matt Tunstall had an interesting bear experience in late August of 1992. He was collecting trash at the various picnic sites in the Porkies. He had stopped at the Mead Mine Site area and started to pick up a trash receptacle from underneath the large old apple tree there. As soon as he touched the trash can, he heard a noise above him in the apple tree. It was a smallish bear, probably a yearling, about eight feet away from him.

Matt decided to return to the park pickup truck from which he watched the bruin for awhile. It came down out of the tree and went into the tall grass at the edge of the clearing. There it stopped and turned around. Sitting in the weeds with just its head showing above them, it scouted the area to make sure there was no danger. Matt was very still and quiet in the truck, so the bear was no longer disturbed by him. It came out of the weeds and started to eat grass at the edge of the clearing. Then it cleaned itself and rolled in the grass. After rolling for a bit, it stopped on its back and sunned its belly for a few minutes.

Matt enjoyed just watching the bear, but he did have to get the trash collected. He opened the truck door, and as soon as he did so, the little bear disappeared into the woods.

SCHIZO THE WONDER BEAR

The very same day that Matt Tunstall was enjoying watching a small bear in the Porkies, some other people were not enjoying watching a big bear elsewhere in the Park. This incident involved a group of fourteen backpackers from a bible school who had set up at a Mirror Lake area campsite. The first child to spot the bear was heeding nature's call in the woods. When the boy pushed aside a branch to go further from camp, he was almost nose to nose with the bear. This poor lad was shocked and frightened, and he ran back to camp to warn his companions. Due to the schizoid behavior of this bear, I shall refer to him in this story as Schizo.

Shortly afterwards, Schizo himself ambled into camp, as was his way. The leader of the bible camp group surprised Schizo by blasting him with a compressed air horn from about forty feet away. Schizo, disgruntled, turned and left. Schizo had never experienced an air horn before. What the heck, people were always trying to scare him away so it wasn't that surprising any more really. The group leader should have waited until Schizo was really close for this type of treatment because it might have been more effective. As it was, Schizo regained his composure and returned very quickly to continue his raid. He was not further deterred by the leader regardless of how much the air horn was used.

Since the group had planned to stay only one night in the interior of the Park, they had brought some food which most people would not consider suitable for backpacking purposes, such as hot dogs and hamburgers. They got into the camp area late but before sunset. They laid their gear down helter skelter strewn all around the big site, then proceeded to cook and prepare to eat. Thus, when Schizo unexpectedly appeared at this time, they were ill prepared for the ensuing encounter.

Schizo's forte at getting food was to approach while campers had gear spread all over with the food just set down in preparation to eat, just like this group. He was not much of a night time sneak around type bear which clandestinely stole food caches from the trees. He was not even especially good at getting food out of the trees. No, Schizo was much more bold and macho than that. He actually preferred daylight operations.

So, once again he did his normal thing, if such a thing can be referred to as normal. Schizo went into the camp and took everything. Now, how does a bear "take everything" - especially from a group of 14 people? Does the bear quickly run around and pick everything up and run off with it? No, obviously not. Schizo would not let the campers touch or pick up anything even though it was theirs. If anyone tried, Schizo was instantly there, and his presence alone was more than enough to discourage even the hardiest backpacker. After all, one does not have to be foolhardy to be hardy. Rangers refer to such situations as bears "taking everything." Now you know.

The fourteen members of the bible camp group fled their campsite in fear and disarray heading towards the Mirror Lake 8 Bunk Cabin. There, Gar Thomas and his son were out in the middle of the Park staying at the cabin that night. The Thomases could not stand idly by when the bible camp group came along just at sunset and without any food or gear. The backpackers' group leader explained what had befallen them and the Thomases let the group stay with them in the cabin.

The next day everyone went over early to the campsite for an inspection. It looked somewhat like a war zone, as everything was torn up.

THE LAST OF THE BEAR RAIDS

An attentive reader will note that several of the incidents described above as occurring previously in 1992 around the Mirror Lake area involved a bear which matches the description and operational methods of Schizo. Undoubtedly, many of the problems that summer near Mirror Lake, Lake of the Clouds (where Schizo sometimes followed retreating parties of backpackers), and the Big Carp River Trail / Correction Line Trail junction, were caused by Schizo.

The following incident, the last one I will give for 1992, was most likely also caused by the same bruin. It occurred on September 4th. The Shaw party had set up camp just across the bridge below the Lake of the Clouds Overlook. A bear entered the camp and took everything. Sound familiar? It was probably Schizo, who was in the area after following hikers north from the Mirror Lake area.

The bear was very bold, and the campers decided to depart leaving everything behind (because the bear had taken it.) The Shaw party managed to borrow a tent from the Park so they could camp elsewhere in the park for that night. They apparently retrieved the remains of their gear the following day. They of course lost all of their food, about $50 worth, and suffered approximately $100 damage to their equipment.

1993

DEMOLITION BEAR

This incident occurred at the Pictured Rocks National Lakeshore near Munising, Michigan. I am indebted to Sheldon Buckmaster of Petoskey, Michigan for the details.

Mr. Buckmaster was a chaperon for a group of Petoskey area students who were on a backpacking trip at the National Lakeshore with their instructor, John Heinzelman. The following young men made up the camping group: Bert Ralston, Don Smith, James Smith, Pat Ecker, Rob Reiter, Jeff Gretch, and Craig Riley. They had left the Grand Marais end of the Park on May 17th with plans to reach the Munising end on May 21st. On the evening of the 20th, just after camp was set up, dinner was eaten, and Sheldon was getting ready to hang the food bag over the cable which the National Park Service provides, a bear came into sight. This bear was later described by rangers as probably a two year old.

John instructed Sheldon to get the food hung right away, which was accomplished. The bear trotted right into camp with some of the group members taking pictures of it. It went right to one of the tent areas and started smelling and swatting over the backpacks sitting there. Then it went to the tent and jumped on top of it. After flattening that tent, it went to the other tent site and started smelling the packs. It knocked over the first one, which was Sheldon's, then spent some time with its head inside of John's pack. It located a plastic bottle filled with gorp, but was unable to do more than put puncture holes all over the container.

It was fairly late and was getting darker. When the bear started damaging equipment, some of the young men as well as John climbed a large fir tree. The bear returned to the first tent area and started to work on Bert's pack. Bert then remembered he left two loaves of honey nut bread in zippered pockets of his pack. The bear took awhile to get these out. While the bear was thus occupied, everyone in the tree except Jeff climbed down.

After devouring the two loaves of nut bread, the bear came towards the group who had retreated into the woods towards Lake Superior.

John ordered everyone towards the beach about 100 yards away. They ran through underbrush and swamp until they were on the beach near the mouth of the Mosquito River. The bear followed them out onto the beach. John had the six young men get under an old rowboat which was on the beach and told them to hold it down.

The bear went directly to the boat and proceeded to sniff and dig around the edges. Meanwhile, the chaperones picked up rocks and sticks and proceeded to throw them at the bear. It was hit a couple of times from about thirty yards away. When this happened, the bear rushed towards John and Sheldon, who crossed the Mosquito River to avoid the bear's wrath. The bear sat on the river's edge, then went to another overturned old boat under which one of the boys had hid for awhile previously.

The bear sniffed around this boat, climbed on top, sat for awhile and then went back into the woods towards the group's camp. By now it was dark out. Sheldon and John both had flashlights, and now and then the bear's eyes could be seen, but every large object, such as the boulders, looked like animals to the unnerved campers. John and Sheldon put themselves back to back and returned to the boat area. Then they had a pow wow with the kids about what to do.

It was decided to build three large fires on the beach a few hundred yards away from the rivermouth and stay there rather than walk nine miles in the dark. There was ample fuel for the fires from all of the driftwood along the shoreline, and everyone pitched in to help. John returned to the campsite to get Jeff, who was still in the top of the fir tree. When John and Jeff returned to the group on the beach, it was estimated that about two and a half hours had passed since the first sighting of the bear.

One of the young men had a medical sugar problem. Another had a candy bar in his pocket. It was decided to give the candy to the young man with the sugar problem. Then everyone tried to get some sleep surrounded by the three large fires.

When it was possible to see in the morning, John noticed some fishermen near the rivermouth. One of the fishermen offered to give Sheldon a ride to the Munising end of the Park to retrieve the group's van after learning of their ordeal. When the camp area was inspected, it was discovered that all of their equipment had been treated the same way by the bear. All packs were knocked over and all tents were flat.

Sheldon retrieved the van and picked up the rest of the group at the Chapel parking lot which was about 1 3/4 miles away from the camp site. After the incident was reported to the National Park

Service, two Rangers were sent out to the camping area. They cooked some bacon, which is one of those things a bear cannot resist. Sure enough, the bear promptly came to visit. The Rangers repeatedly attempted to scare the bear away by spraying it with bear repellent, but the persistent animal kept coming back after them. They decided its behavior was so abnormal that it should be destroyed and were prepared with a shotgun to carry that out.

The bear involved was believed to have been a cub the previous year. Rangers thought that it was probably raised by a mother which picked on backpackers and had taught it to depend on backpackers for food. It should be noted that Hershey bars in the pocket and nut bread loaves in packs will entice a bear into a camp. This bear probably had lots of similar goodies the previous summer from the campers, which caused it to prefer sugar containing items to the natural foods which it would normally depend upon for survival.

The group made it back to Petoskey safely, and each member had a hair raising story to tell when they got home.

1993 PORKIES BEAR STORIES

POOH BEAR

1993 started off with some fairly early bear problems at the Porkies. One of the earliest reports originated from Ranger James Richardson. He had been to the Mirror Lake area around May 12th and reported that a bear had damaged the pit toilets at the Rustic Cabins located there.

Jim's report was short and to the point. "Bear tore up Mirror Lake 2, 4, & 8 bunk cabins' pit toilets. Ripped back wall to access the hole. P.U.!"

The bear had actually gone into the pit toilet bottoms. This was certainly not a normal occurrence. I cannot recall it happening before. This was one bear which any camper would have been able to identify strictly by its smell after this incident.

Being an optimist, I always try to look at the good side of any occurrence. To me the glass of water described in the optimism/pessimism example is not half empty, but at least half full. So what kind of moral can be squeezed out of this story? Well, for all those campers who have ever had a bear come into their camp and tear things up, just be thankful that it was not Pooh Bear.

BEAR RAID ZONE

Mike Rupiper of the Madison based Hoofer's Outing Club lost some equipment to a bear on May 31, 1993. While setting up camp and cooking dinner in the Mirror Lake area, a bear ran into camp and grabbed a pack which it hauled away. The party members started hanging up gear, but the bear came back again and took another pack. It approached within twenty feet of the people and was not afraid, but it did not menace the campers. It also took dog food which was in the dog's pack. Mike's pack had a Pentax single lens reflex camera and his wallet in it. The campers were not able to locate the missing packs even though they searched around for them. Apparently, something in these packs attracted the bear's attention.

CAN'T TOUCH THIS

It was a fairly typical early June day in 1993. I checked the bear trap at the Union Bay Campground Office, and it appeared that the trap's door was down. Sure enough, there was a good sized bear in the trap. A pickup truck with trailer hitch was obtained in order to haul the bear away. On the return to the campground, there were quite a few spectators around watching the trap. Jim Richardson, one of the Porkies Rangers who came to see the bear asked, "What are you going to do about the cubs?" Up in a tree next to the trap were two little cubs.

Well, this definitely complicated the matter. The sow could not just be hauled away and the little cubs left behind. So there was a Rangers' conference on possibilities. The possibility of cutting down the tree, which was mostly dead, was brought up. Then Dave Peloso, a long time Maintenance Mechanic, offered to try and snare the cubs by the foot. It was decided that this was the most likely method to capture the cubs successfully.

First, the trap with the sow was removed from this area. Then, a tractor with a hydraulic bucket was brought to the scene and a long snare was prepared. Dave and I were lifted up high against the trunk of the tree. While Dave tried to get the snare into position, I watched. This did not go well. The snare pole was so long that Dave had a hard time keeping it where he wanted it. Besides, the cubs kept moving around. Also, there was a crowd of campers watching the scene unfold.

This went so slowly, and I got such a sore neck trying to watch what Dave was doing that I forgot to wait until Dave gave the signal to pull on the snare cord. The first time Dave actually got the snare all the way on the closest cubs rear paw, I pulled the snare. The cub pulled his foot out of the snare and climbed further up into the tree making more attempts impossible.

The mother bear was finally released in hopes that it would leave the area with its cubs and not return. This was expecting way too much from a bear used to raiding the garbage dumpster though. The same sow was caught again about two days later. This time the cubs were across the road in a much higher Aspen tree. Once again, there was a conference on possibilities. Again, the sow was removed to the park's service area. The Porkies Auto Mechanic, Jerry Monk, was at the scene this time. He tried simply talking to the bear cubs. The cubs made cute little noises; and, lo and behold, they started climbing backwards down the tree. Jerry succeeded in getting them to come right down to him.

When the first cub was just above Jerry, he grabbed it by the back legs and pulled it off the tree trunk. Jerry was wearing long welder's gloves when he tried this. The little cub curled into the fetal position which placed its mouth and front paws in perfect position to claw and chew on Jerry's hands and arms. Even with the thick leather gloves, Jerry felt the fury of the cubs sharp teeth and claws. The cub also managed to tear his shirt sleeves.

The other little cub was almost within grabbing range right as the first one was seized by Jerry. Someone yelled for another employee (who had regular leather gloves on, not welding gloves) to grab the other cub, which was now grasping the tree trunk with one front paw. The other front paw was making quick little slashing motions which were so fast it looked like a little buz saw. The employee with the regular leather gloves said, "I'm not touching that thing!"

The scrappy little menace which had been seized was next placed inside of a full sized live bear trap. Then the bear traps containing the sow and the cub were positioned so that the two sliding trap doors were together. Next, the framework on the two traps was chained together so that the traps could not be moved apart. After this, both trap doors were raised a little. It did not take any encouragement on the part of the park employees to get the cub to immediately scoot under the two trap doors into its mother's trap. Then the doors were lowered and the traps separated.

Unfortunately, the other little cub was not captured. The mother was such a problem that it was decided to remove her to a new area with only the one cub. The plan was to capture the other cub as soon as possible and then take it to the new area also.

GRUMPY OLD BEARS

On June 22nd, there were a couple of Porkies backpacker bear reports. At the Big Carp River Shelter area, a group stored their food in the shelter while they made preparations to hang it. They took too long though because a bear showed up during this time period. The group decided to leave, and the bear followed them for a bit. It then returned to the shelter, tore screening off to gain access, and ate half of their food. The group had to leave three days earlier than planned.

This reminds me of something regarding the Adirondack style shelters in Great Smokey Mountains National Park. Someone told me that one of the methods of keeping food from the bears there was to place it against the back wall of the shelter with the packers sleeping in front of it. This way the bears would have to go over or through the backpackers to reach their food. From what has occurred at the Porkies shelters, that method does not seem to be overly desirable to me.

At another location and the same date, a 200 pound bear entered the camp and took the food pack which also contained a wallet. The food had not been hung yet. The backpack was later found, but the wallet was not.

The next day, a small bear jumped on a tent at the Little Carp Rivermouth area. The tent had people in it when this occurred. There were puncture marks and a hole in the tent. The bear was successful at getting a food cache out of the tree which was up about 20 feet high. It turns out that the bear was a finicky eater. It ate only sweet things according to Paulette Aho, the Park's Office Manager.

On June 26th, there was an occurrence well out of the ordinary. Ranger Ellis Fryer noticed a bear hanging around a car parked at the Little Carp River Road. The bear was not a large one. As Ellis approached, the bear went a short distance into the woods, but it did not leave. It grunted and popped its jaws at Ellis, indicating great displeasure at being interrupted. Ellis attempted to scare the bear away, but he was not successful. A rear window of the car was laying on the ground, as well as a piece of padding. There were bear prints all over the car. Inside, on the back seat within easy reach of the bear was a large amount of food items.

On the 30th, a YMCA group from Spring, Wisconsin had an encounter with a large bear around 6:30 AM. The bear came into camp, jumped on a tent bending the poles, inspected the packs, tried to get at the group's hung food, and stuck its paw through the wall of the counselor's tent, not necessarily all in that order. The members of the group finally yelled at the bear and it left.

Our next Porkies report came from a Hudsonville, Wisconsin couple who were day hiking on the Government Peak Trail near Trap Falls on July 6th. They noticed that a bear weighing an estimated 300 pounds or more was following them. They yelled at the bruin and it retreated briefly, then it followed them again. The couple went right into the Upper Carp River, then quickly left the area. The bear ceased following them. The bear never got closer than about forty feet from the hikers, who were carrying no food or packs of any kind, but who had recently eaten at the End of the Rainbow Restaurant. Perhaps their clothing still retained enough food smell from the restaurant to attract the bear.

On the following day, Summer Ranger Paula Simmons reported that a large bear was following, bothering and getting food from many campers and packers near the bridge below the Lake of the Clouds overlook. It appears that following people was becoming a new specialty method for bears to help separate park users from their food. After all, a large bear following one out in the forest is not exactly the most pleasant thing that could happen on an outing.

UP CLOSE AND WAY TOO PERSONAL

Summer Ranger Tricia Rigoni recorded a typical bear incident with a somewhat unusual twist which occurred on July 9th, 1993. A bear raided a YMCA group camped near the North Mirror Lake Trail bridge below Lake of the Clouds Scenic Area. This bear was clearly used to people and good at getting food from them. It was described as very bold, which usually means that it was not afraid to come close to people. In this incident, the bear trotted up to a 12 year old boy, stuck its nose right into his belly, and gave him several good sniffs. The bear then went to each tent door where the other group members were watching the action and sniffed at them.

Then the bruin climbed the tree with the group's food bag in it, broke the branch on which it was hung and jumped out to tear the bottom out of the bag. The bear managed to get all of the group's food from that one bag and did about $20 worth of damage to the equipment. The group lost three days worth of food for 12 people. Try to imagine eating a meal consisting of a dozen people's food for three days. Probably very filling. Now you know why the bears prefer backpacking groups rather than hunting for berries.

I suspect that the young lad who had the bear sniff his belly no longer goes backpacking. This story brings to mind an incident which occurred to me one time when I was registering a motor home in the off season at Union Bay Campground. I walked quickly around the monster sized vehicle to knock on the door only to find myself facing a huge sheep dog which suddenly stood up right in front of me. It growled for some time with its mouth about five inches from my lower belly. Finally, its owner came out and saved me from a possibly terrible fate. I am much more careful while registering camps nowdays.

THE REST OF THE STORY

On the 11th of July, 1993, an out of the ordinary event took place at the Summit Peak Scenic Area parking lot. A bear got into the garbage truck and started tearing up the trash bags which were being hauled from the outer areas of the park to the dumpsters at the Union Bay Service Area.

Summer Ranger Matt Harter had stopped to clean the toilet building at that location. While he was busy at the toilet building, a bear weighing about 100 pounds climbed right into the bed of his park pickup truck and did what bears do best. Matt radioed the Park Headquarters to report what was going on. The Park had recently obtained some bear repellant spray which the management wanted to test for effectiveness in various situations. So I was given a spray can and sent out to repel the invading bruin.

Upon my arrival at the Summit Peak parking lot, the bear was spotted right in the back of Matt's pickup truck tearing up garbage bags. I parked on the far side of the area and sneaked across the lot towards his truck. The bear looked up a couple of times at me and the third time stopped what it was doing to take a good look at me. I was about twenty feet away and was frozen in my spot as soon as the bear's head turned my way. When it looked down, I ducked down to be more out of its sight and sneaked right up to the truck.

The bear looked my way again when my outstretched hand with the spray was about 5 or 6 feet away. I got in a good spray in at the bear's head, and it immediately turned, jumped out of the truck bed and ran away down the parking lot road towards the west. It slowed to a walk as it entered the woods on the west end of the lot. I followed. The bear went down into a gully, up the other side to a high area and followed the top of the ridge to the north and east. I turned around and went back to the parking lot and the truck.

When I reached the truck, here was the bear on top of the bank right in front of it. It beat me back there by following the Beaver Creek Trail and coming down from north of the toilet building. It was going to go right back into the pickup as soon as I got out of the way. I decided to try and hide between the garbage pickup and a custom van which was parked next to it. Hopefully, the bear would go around behind the van and when it went between the two vehicles, I would nail it again from my hidden location.

Bears are not quite that dense, however. I was not any more hidden from the bear than a frog which goes to the bottom of a pond in plain sight is hidden from someone who disturbs it. The bear was well aware of exactly where I was. It could probably see my feet looking under the van even though I tried to stay beside the rear wheel. When the bear came around the back towards the pickup, it was not anywhere near the vehicles or me, but way out in the road, too far away to spray again.

So I decided to just stay there and keep the bear away from the truck. The only problem with this was that I could not stay there forever. Matt indicated that this bear had been hanging around the Summit Peak lot for several days, getting into the trash cans every day and making a mess. What was needed was another spray located much more directly in the bear's face to test whether it would be useful at altering undesirable bear behaviors.

I went into the woods in the middle of the parking lot's circular road. Taking up position behind a huge hemlock tree which was directly behind the left rear corner of the garbage pickup, I patiently waited. There were a fair number of park visitors around watching the bear from a distance, some taking videos. Somewhere, someone has video of what occurred.

Slowly and very cautiously the bear returned to the truck. It came from the west, climbing onto the left rear corner of the truck bed and put its forepaws down into the garbage while keeping its rear legs up on the corner of the truck. I watched what it was going to do. Every now and then it would pause and look around but did this less frequently as time went on. It seemed that it would be possible when it had its head down in the truck bed to sneak up directly behind it. The next time its head went down, I scurried to a position behind the bear with the bear spray in my right hand held as far away from me as possible.

I ended up directly behind the bear with the spray can only 12 inches from its rear end. It was definitely a male. The bear had no idea that I was behind it getting ready to spray it again. When this location was reached, the bear once again stopped and looked around, but it did not try to look behind itself. It looked to the right and left and went back to digging through garbage and did not notice me directly behind it only one foot away.

I held the spray can in my fully extended arm and slowly sidestepped to my right, keeping the can about 12 inches away from the bear. As I came around from behind it, I aimed directly at its head so, if it turned, it would receive the spray full in the eyes and nose. I was able to get almost all the way to the opposite corner of the pickup before the bear turned its head toward me. It received a good dose of the repellant, turned away from me, stumbled while jumping out of the truck bed, and trotted away to the west again, but this time with noticeable amounts of saliva running out of its mouth.

This particular bear spray is made from cayenne peppers and has a noticeable red color. It is not dangerous, causing only temporary discomforture which wears off about twenty minutes after. The bear repeated its previous route into the woods but instead of going up the other side of the gully and back towards the truck, it went very slowly down the gully and away from the area. The bear kept stopping with fluids dripping from its nose and mouth. It obviously received a good dose of the repellant this time. The bear did not return to the Summit Peak lot as far as we know during 1993.

Now for the rest of the story. To the Park visitors who witnessed the above occurrences, it undoubtedly looked like the Rangers were well equipped, organized, knowledgeable, and confident in dealing with that dog-gone bear. In reality, however, things did not seem that way to the two Rangers who were involved.

Approaching bears is not recommended. So, approaching a bear to chase it out of a truck or to spray it runs against the grain for people with normal common sense. I usually classify myself as someone with normal common sense.

This was the first time the park had tested this spray on a bear. It was not known how the bear would react to the spray. I was not overly confident about this. While approaching the bear to spray it, it seemed to me that there was a good possibility the bear might turn around and attempt to plant a paw full of claws on my arm or face. And of course, after it was sprayed, what then? Would it run away, or would it become mean and nasty and attempt to put perforations in me? I was not confident at all about any of this. Everything ended well, but the Rangers were not anywhere near as confident and competent as it may have appeared to the visitors watching and making videotapes.

UNDER SIEGE

July 12th turned out to be a very memorable day for several groups camping near the Mirror Lake area. They got to meet Habeeb, a scizoid bear named by Ranger Mike Rafferty. Habeeb and Schizo the Wonder Bear from the previous year were undoubtedly the very same bear. Let us continue to use the name Habeeb for this year. There were about sixteen people in four different groups of campers who were to experience Habeeb this day.

Our story starts where one group's leader was attempting to hang up the last bag of their food at the designated campsite on the south side of the lake. Suddenly, Habeeb showed up. Habeeb wanted that food. He rushed right up to the leader, who jumped out of the way and fell on a rock outcropping injuring his knee. Habeeb ate this bag of food and tried unsuccessfully to get another group's food which was well hung.

The campers all grabbed their packs and left the designated campsite area. They headed for the north side of the lake. Habeeb followed the campers and periodically charged one or another of them. They crossed the bridge at the lake's outlet and went to the east towards the cabins. Habeeb kept following and charging. The bear would charge a camper forcing him to drop his pack and then would ignore the pack and charge a different camper. When the campers got to the clearing around the Mirror Lake 8 Bunk Cabin, they decided to try something different. Habeeb was still on their heels charging at them now and then.

Habeeb had already bothered some other campers who had broken into the unoccupied cabin. While Habeeb charged a couple of the straggling campers, everyone else found some kind of refuge at the cabin area. Some of the campers climbed up on the roof of the cabin. Some went into the cabin. Several got into one of the rowboats and rowed out into the lake. The stragglers ran into the pit toilet near the cabin. Then and only then was everyone safe from Habeeb.

After waiting quite a while without seeing Habeeb, a couple of campers came out of hiding to try and get their gear and to leave the area. No sooner did they start out than Habeeb appeared and charged them. The campers attempted to leave their various shelters several times, and each time the bear would suddenly appear and charge these hardy souls.

Eventually, the campers were able to leave their temporary fortresses, gather their scattered gear, and leave the park. Habeeb, not particularly adept at getting food which was well hung, relocated to the Section 17 Cabin area along the Little Carp River Trail. It was a good thing he did too because the powers that be decided he was due to be disposed of permanently. An attempt was made the very next night to catch Habeeb in the act at the South Mirror Lake Campsite, but Habeeb made himself scarce at Mirror Lake.

The campers in the Section 17 Cabin area were not too pleased about Habeeb's change of location though. The occupants of the cabin reported that Habeeb terrorized backpackers between the Little Carp River Road and the first mile of the Cross Trail. He went after packs by charging people, forcing them to drop the packs. The campers had to take shelter with the cabin occupants because they had no gear and it was late. Habeeb came around the cabin regularly between 6 and 8 PM and also between 6 and 8 AM.

Once it was determined that Habeeb could probably be located in this area, a new team was sent out to destroy this bear. On the night of July 19, a backpacker, Edward Baetzold, volunteered to help Ranger Ellis Fryer locate the bear which had been terrorizing camps for months and probably for years. The Baetzold party reported that Habeeb was destroyed never to terrorize again. Unfortunately, while they were out looking for Habeeb, a different bear went to Edward's camp and ate all of his food.

A BEAR TALE WITH A HAPPY ENDING

On July 17, the Porkies Headquarters received a report of a bear cub hit by a car near the Union Mine Trailhead on South Boundary Road. Park Auto Mechanic Jim Rogan and I responded to this report. We took a large plastic trash can with cover and a 3 pound hammer just in case either was needed. When we arrived at the scene, Summer Ranger Matt Harter was waiting for us. The cub was sitting on the shoulder of the road.

I was concerned that the mother would show up suddenly while we were attempting to examine the cub and make us regret being there. So, I asked Matt to watch one side of the road while I kept an eye on the other so Jim could check out the little fella. The road sides were steep and filled with thick underbrush which could easily conceal the mother bear.

The cub was wide awake but unable to move. As we approached, it tried to turn and leave but stopped, possibly due to pain. It made no further attempts to get away even though it was apparent that it did not like us nearby. It could still hiss and bare its sharp teeth.

We were discussing the appropriate action to take in this kind of case. If the cub had been injured so seriously that recovery was not possible, we would have put it out of its misery. That is what the 3 pound hammer was for. There were no visible signs of injury to the cub. Perhaps this little falla could be saved.

I radioed the local Conservation Officer, Jackie Strauch, concerning our little bear. She advised that we should put it into a container and bring it to the Headquarters where she would pick it up. That is what the trash can was for. We placed the can upside down over the cub and slid the cover underneath of it. Then we righted the can and put it into our pickup truck.

When Jackie arrived to pick up the cub, she indicated that there was a veterinarian who was willing to work on wildlife and that she had people who would attempt to nurse the cub back to health. The cub did recover completely. It was released in the same general area where it was found on approximately July 27 of 1993.

FROM DUSK TILL DAWN

With the demise of Habeeb, there were a lot fewer bear incidents during the rest of 1993, but there were still some other problem bears around. After Habeeb left Mirror Lake, another bear filled the void he left. While this other bear was very bold, it was not into charging people. It simply came around the camps and tried to get their food caches out of the trees, usually at night.

It may have been fairly successful at this on occasion, but the party who reported this bear on August 26th did not lose their food to it. They indicated that it kept going from camp to camp along the shoreline of Mirror Lake trying to get food from the camps there. One of its methods for trying to get down food bags was to chew on the branches where they were hung. It kept going back and forth from camp to camp and chewing on branches all night long, and the campers got little sleep that night.

WHILE YOU WERE SLEEPING

The Shrane party from Skandia, Michigan got a surprise on the night of September 4th, 1993. They were apparently camped near the Correction Line Trail junction with the Big Carp River Trail. During the night their dog scared a bear out of camp. In the process, the surprised bear ran over the Shrane's tent with them inside of it. The bear continued to hang around their campsite until it was finally successful at getting their food out of a tree. It also got a neighboring camp's food. At least, if the bear gets your food, you get some shut-eye afterwards.

OUT ON A LIMB

On September 25th, a large bear investigated the camp of the Palmquist party. The bear went out on the food cache branch and broke it right off the tree, thus getting their food supply. It also investigated the campers who were in sleeping bags but without a tent. The bear clawed at one of the bags ripping it. I wonder if the Palmquists have given up backpacking yet? I would.

WHERE THE RIVERS FLOW NORTH

The final Porkies story for 1993 involved a camp at the junction of the Government Peak Trail and the Union Spring Trail. The Jamison party took precautions making sure that their food, as well as their Coleman Peak stove, was actually hanging out over the upper Big Carp River. A bear managed to get their stash down anyway. The stove in a nylon stuff stack was never located.

1994

IT'S A BAD, BAD, BAD, BAD YEAR!

1994 was the worst year ever for backpackers in Porcupine Mountains State Park, at least as far as black bear problems go anyway. There were 111 bear incident reports filed this year, compared to 35 reports for 1992, 64 reports for 1993 and 44 reports the following year. Many of the 1994 reports filed mention problems for several camps, not just one. Some also mention incidents which occurred to other camps which were never reported by the camps involved. There were bears everywhere throughout the park picking on backpackers trying to get their food. My initial statement to backpackers preparing to head out into the Porcupine Mountains in 1994 was, "You are going to lose your food to a bear."

It got so bad in the summer of 1994 that the Park had to take some action to attempt to control the problem in the future. Black Bear Awareness, an organization committed to the study and better understanding of black bears, was contacted and asked for assistance in dealing with the increasing problems. There was a meeting in early December between some of the Park staff and members of the group. Jeff Traska and Bob and Diane Baty represented Black Bear Awareness. Methods to alleviating the problems being experienced were the main point of these discussions.

Jeff Traska did some midsummer backpacking in 1994 to investigate the types of problems the Porkies was experiencing. He stated at the outset of the December meeting that the Porkies does not have a bear problem, it has a people problem. The campers generally have a very poor understanding of black bears and are much too careless with their food and garbage.

The concensus of this meeting was that there was a major educational program needed to inform the park users of the problems that their presence caused for the black bear population. It was also decided that a suggestion should be made to the State Park System to invest in a considerable number of bear poles for the interior of the Park and to replace all trash receptacles in the Park with bear proof models similar to those found in the National Park System.

BEARASSIC PARK

As noted above, there were bear problems everywhere in the Porkies during 1994. Here are just a few of the interesting happenings.

MAY

The problems started early. On May 13th, the Hagerty party from Chicago reported that a bear got their food while they camped near the Big Carp Rivermouth area. The bear apparently climbed a tree and tore the bottom out of their food hanging bag. It also took a backpack which was never found. (There must be a tremendous stash of such backpacks back in the Porkies somewhere.) This bear was somewhat unusual - it had a distinct limp on the right front leg. In fact, the right front leg was wounded, and the bear carried it off of the ground.

On the 23rd of May, a report was received from a backpack camp getting a refund because a bear got all of their food. The bear had climbed the tree and crawled out on a small branch which held up the food stash. The branch broke with the bear, food bag, branch and all falling to the ground. The bear proceeded to eat the food and the food bag. It also ate the camp permit which was in the food bag. This made it a little more difficult for the backpackers to get a refund when they had to leave early due to lack of food.

The next day there was a report from Ranger Pete Kemppainen of a three legged bear in Union Bay Campground which pried a car door open at the Jantz campsite trying to get at food. Someone started referring to this limping bear (or these limping bears?) as "Tripod."

On May 28th, two ladies from the group staying at the Little Carp Cabin complained about a bear limping on a front leg following them along the river. They had to run across the Little Carp on some rocks to get away from the approaching bruin. The bear then followed them downstream on the opposite side of the river until it reached the bridge which is close to the cabin. It then crossed on the bridge and followed the ladies right to the cabin, hanging around outside for a while after they had entered.

Needless to say, these two cabin users were a little upset. They had not been carrying any food. They did have bear repellent spray in their possession, however, so they would not have been entirely defenseless if the bear had gotten too close. Still, this was fairly unusual behavior for a black bear.

On May 29th, just to sort of round out the month, a very large bear entered the Mansfield camp near Mirror Lake and destroyed a $500 tent.

JUNE

On June 2nd, a party of four backpackers camping halfway between the Big Carp and Little Carp Rivermouth areas stayed up all night chasing away bears. The bears had chewed on the tree branch holding their food stash and also on the rope holding the stash. One of the bears was described as particularly large. The members of this party had selected the camping spot to avoid the bear problems they had heard about at the rivermouth areas themselves. Well, I guess its pretty obvious that the bears constantly traverse the one mile of trail between those two areas. So this camp ended up being visited by all the bears from both rivermouth areas.

YOU KNOW WHO AND THE THREE BEARS

Once upon a time, June 2, 1994 to be exact, some Porkies backpackers had a problem with the three bears. Actually it was a problem with three different bears. They had set up camp along the Government Peak Trail. Then during the night, the bears started coming and trying to get their food. The first bear came around at 11:30 PM. It was a smallish bear and was unable to get their food. The next bear was larger. It showed up about 2:30 in the morning. It was unable to get their food.

But the last bear was a lot bigger than the other two. It was larger than the bear on display in the Porkies Visitor Center which weighed 249 pounds. Ambling into camp at about 5:00 AM, it was very successful at getting their food. It also decided to take all of their backpacks and chew on them too, even though the packs did not have food in them. Don't ask me why. Bears are that way sometimes.

THE BEARS OF PORCUPINE MOUNTAINS DO NOT DISCRIMINATE BASED UPON RACE, RELIGION, SEX, NATIONAL ORIGIN, OR MODE OF TRANSPORTATION - THEY'LL EAT ANYONE'S FOOD

On June 6 of 1994 Bob and Veronica Bagshaw of Seattle ran into one of the Porkies black bear bandits. The Bagshaws were on a sea kayaking journey around the United States to benefit the Save the Children Foundation. They will be traveling over 10,000 miles in slightly less than two years. However, their trip came to a screeching halt at the Little Carp Rivermouth area when a bear took their food and damaged their equipment as reported by Rick McVey of the U.S. Forest Service.

The bear first approached a group of backpackers setting around a fire near the rivermouth. It came within eight feet, snorted, and then went towards the Bagshaws' kayaks. Bob and Veronica stood their ground near the kayaks trying to scare the bear away. The bear would have none of it though and continued its approach. When it got to within fifteen feet of the kayakers, they decided to back off. Even though their food was in watertight, airtight containers in sealed cargo areas of their boats, the bear knew it was there. Bears either have a sixth sense about these things, or a really good smeller. What do you think? I vote for the good smeller.

Mr. Bruin tore the covers off of their hatches and got all of their food. The author still has one of these hatch covers with a neat three inch diameter hole bitten into it. The damage to their equipment caused by the bear necessitated the ordering of replacement parts for their kayaks from Seattle, as well as restocking of their food supply (which they probably did AFTER leaving Porcupine Mountains.)

I HATE IT WHEN THAT HAPPENS

The sun was up and there was every indication that June 10, 1995 was going to be a beautiful sunny and warm late spring day. I started a check of the Union Bay Campground by first heading down the lower road along the lakeshore. It was not long before something caught my eye.

At the Versluis' camp on Site Number 21 about halfway along the lake there was a typical camper's screen tent but this one had holes in it. In fact, it had two very large holes in it. These holes were circular, located in the middle of the tent wall, and approximately 2 - 3 feet in diameter. One was on the north side of the screen tent towards the lake, while the other was on the east side away from the Versluis' vehicle and tent trailer.

I continued on with my campground check and returned later to talk with the campers. It turns out that a sow with cubs wandered by on the rocks along the lakeshore around 3:00 AM. The sow came up from the shore and entered the screen tent from that side. The campers woke up and turned on a light to see what was near the screen tent. They startled the bear which left through the east wall of the screen tent. There was no food in the enclosure, just two lawn chairs and the picnic table. There may have been food smells still on the table, or spilled food on the ground which the present campsite occupants were not aware of.

When I first saw the holes, I imagined how easy it would be for a bear to make them. The screen tent would be able to hold back the bear about as well as a spider's web would hold back you or I from going wherever we wanted to go. A bear would simply give it a swat and the paw's five integral knives would create an opening which the bear's body would force out to the necessary size.

Returning to the shoreline campground road in the afternoon, I noticed that the Versluis party had patched the two holes. They apparently used some type of white plastic or waxy paper to fill the void with the old standby, duct tape, to hold it in place. When I was checking the campground early the following morning, the campers had taken defensive measures with the screen tent. Since it was simply draped over a metal frame, they rolled up the sides and tied them at the top. Thus the bears or other inquisitive creatures could wander wheresoever they wanted on the Versluis' site without causing more damage to the screen tent at least.

THESE ARE A FEW
OF THE BEARS' FAVORITE THINGS

A bear managed to get food as well as a candy bar hidden in the first aid kit out of the pack at a camp near the Correction Line Shelter. Exactly why there was food or candy bars inside of someone's pack where a bear could get at it, I do not know. Everyone should know by now that that is a big NO NO. This bear raid occurred on June 6th, and the bear also raided several other camps that night.

According to Ranger Mike Rafferty, the bear showed no fear. Have you ever seen those window stickers in cars and trucks which say - NO FEAR! I think they are supposed to have something to do with team sports. However, whenever I see one of them, it reminds me of certain bears. I get reminded of certain bears more often than I would really like.

In an entirely separate case, a backpack was found out in the Porkies on the 19th of June. It appeared to have been out in the woods a considerable amount of time, since it was completely soaked and smelled of mold so badly that it was a task to keep from gagging near it. Everyone else avoided it like the plague, but it had to be examined and I wanted to find out the story associated with it.

On inspection, it turned out that there was a relatively small hole in the top of the pack which had apparently been made by a bear taking out some food item. Nothing else was torn or damaged by the bear. Apparently, the bear had grabbed the pack and run off with it due to a good smelling morsel inside.

There was nothing good smelling inside any more. There were some horrible smelling clothes items, and there was a Pentax 35mm single lens reflex camera which also smelled pretty bad. It had been wet so long that it was quite rusty. This caused me to revise my estimate of how long it had been out in the woods upward from at least a few weeks to at least a few months.

Then a wallet was located. The pack belonged to a Mike Rupiper of Madison. Every item in this pack smelled so badly of mildew that it was inconceivable that anything could ever be used again. The camera was undoubtedly a complete loss not only due to the rust, but also because of the mildew which permeated every pore and fiber of everything. When not actually inspecting the pack, it had to be kept sealed in a plastic bag or left outside due to the smell.

I contacted the owner to ask if he even wanted this gear back. He did. I warned him that it was in pretty bad shape. It was while discussing its return that the time of loss was discovered. Mike had it taken by the bear over the Memorial Day weekend - in 1993 - more than a year earlier. No wonder it was so wet and stinky! The report of Mike's lost pack is found in *BEAR RAID ZONE,* on page 130.

On June 22nd at the Big Carp Rivermouth area, there was another case of "food items" in backpacks. There the bear got toothpaste and cough drops. It ripped open everyone's pack. Exactly how may packs we don't know for sure, but there must have been several. Come on now, backpackers, you should all know by now that things which smell like food are an open invitation to bears or other animals to damage your equipment trying to get at it. So, do I think all the backpackers are suddenly going to stop doing what they have been doing for years? Not hardly.

CAN'T BEAR THIS

Camp U-NAH-LI-YA had a couple of typical 1994 bear encounters during their several days at the Porkies in late June. "Typical" means they lost their food. This year was clearly turning out to be worse than usual for bears getting backpackers' food. It was so bad that I had started telling all the packers whom I talked to that they would lose their food. I estimate that over 75% of the backpackers had some problems with bears coming around, that around 60% lost some food to bears, and that probably 40% lost all of their food this summer.

There were 10 girls including leaders in the U-NAH-LI-YA camp group. On June 27th, camped somewhere along the Big Carp River Trail, they lost a pack with all of their food to a bear. The bear climbed the tree where they hung the pack and was able to swat the pack causing it to swing around the tree like a tetherball. This made it easy for the bear to then get all the food. It destroyed the pack in the process.

The group left the interior and with some help from Summer Ranger Doug Roberts were able to restock themselves with food from the Silver City General Store. Not to be daunted by little things like bears getting all their food and completely destroying their pack, they went right back out into the Porkies interior to do it all over again. This occurred on June 29th along the Lake Superior Trail about two miles in from Highway M-107. A bear came to camp at about 9:30 PM. It got the food from the tree where it had been hung with care, probably using the same method as the previous bear at the previous location.

Unlike the previous time when the girls stayed in their tents and simply listened to the bear wandering around their site between 10:00 PM and 4:00 AM while it located their food pack, tore it out of the tree and then tore apart their pack and ate all their food, this time the girls sallied forth to scare the bear away. Unfortunately, their sally and scare did not work. The bear did more scaring than the girls did, so the group left their camp
and gear to the bear and went to the Union Bay Campground for the night. I'm not clear on whether they stayed in the toilet building or brought a tent with them. In any event, they went back to the interior site the next day to retrieve their gear.

These incidents were undoubtedly not much fun for the members of the Camp U-NAH-LI-YA group, except perhaps in retrospect. They can look back now and realize they survived the bear incidents of 1994. Hopefully, the leaders will have learned some lessons regarding food handling which will be put to good use if the group returns to bear country in the future.

DAN'S BAKE SALE

On July 12th, 1994, a big bear limping on the right front foot took food out of a cooler which was left outside overnight unattended at site #68 in the Union Bay Campground. This occurred at about 5:00 AM when it was just light enough out to see.

Then on July 26th, a bear with an injured front leg got $90.00 worth of groceries from a similarly situated cooler at site #94 in the same campground. Do you think this bear would be likely to return to Union Bay Campground in search of coolers?

Well, it did. On July 30th, it hit a screen tent and coolers on at least three sites after it surgically removed some food from a tent trailer. It seems that on July 30th, many of the campers lost their common sense or something like that. I distinctly remember one of them the next day saying that he saw someone leave a cooler out so he thought there must not be any problem doing so. Actually, the vast majority of the campers had no problems. It was the ones who left coolers out or food handy who mainly had the problems.

The first thing which happened that night was a bear came out of the woods behind site #57 in Union Bay and passed near the rented tent trailer of Dan Dykhuis. Dan was over at the next site talking to his neighbor, Dave Flokstra. It was 11:00 PM and fairly dark out. Dave noticed a bear over by Dan's tent trailer and mentioned it to Dan. A bear had come out of the woods, stood up on its rear legs next to the screen window on Dan's tent trailer, slashed the screen open, grabbed a loaf of bread and some cookies (which were conveniently placed just inside the screen window for safekeeping) and ran off with them into the woods. I imagine the bear then spent a minute or two gulping down the goodies, bags and all, and then went wandering elsewhere around the campground looking for other campers who were as tempting with their food as Dan had been.

I talked to Dan's party the next day. They were amazed and shaken that a bear would and could take things out of their tent trailer. Screen is not much of a barrier. In this case, Dan had left the large windows open on both sides of the tent trailer with just the screens keeping out bugs and other things. There was a warm moderate westerly breeze right through Dan's trailer carrying the smell of his bread and cookies out into the surrounding area. We must remember that some of the things outside of our tents and tent trailers are bigger and more powerful than mere bugs. The screen is to keep out bugs. When tempted by campers with good smelling bread and cookies, what bear would be able to resist snatching them from one inch beyond a barrier equivalent to a cobweb? Dan really set himself up well for what occurred.

I spent some time trying to calm the Dykhuises down so they would not feel that the bear was sure to come back and snack on them the next time. The simple solution is to put all food away in sealed containers. If there is anything particularly smelly, seal it and put it in a clean cooler locked in the vehicle (as long as the vehicle is not a convertible.) Also, it is advisable to plan before going camping on which foods to take and how to keep food smells to a minimum.

Well, that bear left Dan's site and wandered all around Union Bay that night. It took a cooler from under the picnic table on site #63 and ate that food. It pulled a cooler out from under the tongue of a tent trailer on another site and ate that food, and it got into a couple of other coolers too.

Apparently, one of the last things it did before heading back out into the woods was to stop at site #8 around 4:00 AM. It tore a hole right next to the doorway of the screen tent belonging to the Hinze party. They did not have any food inside of their screen tent, but there were a cooler and some Rubbermaid containers in the tent which the bear could not resist checking out just in case. Thus ended ALL COOLERS NIGHT at Union Bay.

THE CHAMPAIGN BOYS

On August 9 of 1994, there was a very persistent bear which bothered a Champaign, Illinois, Boy Scout group camped near Mirror Lake. The 15 scouts tried repeatedly to scare this bear away, but were unsuccessful. The bear climbed several trees and got the scouts' food. This was just one more typical occurrence for summertime at the Porkies. The only difference between this summer and others was that in 1994 there were literally hundreds of such incidents.

CABIN BUSTERS

Also on August 9th, a different bear got food from the Wuille party camped somewhere out near the Buckshot Cabin on the Lake Superior Trail. This bear was wounded in the right front paw. It climbed what must have been a fairly small food tree by bending it over and getting the food. The camping party evacuated their campground, went to Buckshot Cabin and broke into it. They stayed there until the following morning.

SNACK, CRAPPLE, POK

There were a couple of bear incidents on August 27th, 1994, which were not necessarily completely out of the ordinary but were interesting. On the lower Big Carp River a bold bear got a camp's food bag which was hung out over the river and tied off on shore. It simply bit the tie rope off and retrieved the food bag from the water. All of the camp's food for their second day and night of camping was lost. Believe me, there were numerous camps which lost all or most of their food to bears that summer.

As for locating the food hanging rope, more than one backpacker has described how a bear has come into camp and started to look around in the trees overhead to see where the food is hung. When a bear exhibits behavior like this, waltzing into camp and stargazing, you can be assured that it is also good at getting the food out of the tree once it is located. The above bear came back after finishing off the food and dragged two packs out of the vestibule of the campers' tent during the night.

In the other incident that same night, a party at Mirror Lake met two different bears at different times with different techniques. The smaller bear to visit camp, approximately a 150 pounder, was very used to people, and stopped by several times to check out the campers' gear. In the very early morning a much larger bear came and took off into the woods with a pack which contained no food. When located the following morning, it was discovered that the bear had chewed up everything - the pack, the stove, the water bottles and everything else which had been in the pack.

HYUNDAI HEAVEN

The young couple from Chicago came to the Porcupine Mountains Wilderness State Park to get away from it all. They succeeded. Way out in the interior, near the beautiful Shining Cloud Falls, they made their camp. The food supply was hung over a smallish branch to discourage a bear from climbing out after it.

Then a very large bear came, broke the whole branch right off the tree and took their food. The bear also got the key to their rented Hyundai car. Without food and unable to get into their car if they returned to it, the couple decided to head towards the Presque Isle end of the Park to seek assistance and make a call to the car rental firm. Upon arrival at Presque Isle, they discovered that there is not even a phone available on the remote west end of the Porkies.

So, the couple then hitchhiked to the east end of the Park to the Union Bay Campground. They obtained a campsite. Then they called the rental agency. As I recall, a friendly clerk told them that there was a code in the glove compartment of the Hyundai which would allow a new key to be made. The clerk told the camper that all he needed to do was take the code number for the car, go to any nearby place which makes keys, get a Hyundai blank and have a new key made from the code numbers.

The camper told the clerk that he was locked out of the car and could not get the code. He was told to call back later. I advised them that places which make keys in the western Upper Peninsula of Michigan are not very likely to have Hyundai key blanks on hand. There probably was not a Hyundai blank within a hundred miles or more of where we were. Also, there are probably not any places which can make such a key from the code within a considerable distance. It would be much easier for the rental company to simply send them a replacement key.

The campers had to get some necessities - you know, food. They decided to walk to Silver City and call the rental agency when they returned. After calling the company again, they still did not get anyone who understood the predicament which they were in. They were told to call back later.

I advised them to ask for a supervisor and to explain that they were not in the Chicago area, but in a relatively backward wilderness area. They did this and were told to call back the next day to speak with a particular person at the company.

I once again advised them to make their situation extremely clear to a person who had some authority to make a decision at the rental agency. Make sure to point out that their only key was gone, that a blank key was not available, that the vehicle was stranded way up here in Michigan, that they were stranded far from the vehicle at a State Park campground. I also advised them to ask the person in authority what the rental company wanted them to do with the company's car - leave it where it was, break into it, or what? Let the company decide what to do about the company's stranded car.

Someone at the rental company finally decided to "overnight" them a key by Federal Express, and they left the campground and the Park the following day to return to the Chicago area.

I'LL FOLLOW YOU ANYWHERE

On the Labor Day weekend of 1994, a couple took their 5 year old daughter to the Mirror Lake area for a day hike. They traveled light - the little girl had a bright pink fanny pack which she was thrilled to wear. Other than that, they had no gear. The weather was beautiful, and they had a wonderful hike in. As expected, the Mirror Lake area was enchanting.

On their trek back out along the South Mirror Lake Trail, the father noticed that a black bear was following behind them back about fifty yards. It was relatively easy to see because most of the South Mirror Lake Trail is actually a road bed. The father didn't worry too much about the bear because he knew that bears do not normally bother people.

As the couple and their small daughter continued on, the bear just followed along. After a while, it became apparent that the bear was following faster than the trio of day hikers was walking. The bear was gaining on them. So, the hikers picked up their speed. This increase did not help them, though, as the bear continued to gain on them slowly.

By now, the father was beginning to worry about the situation. His 5 year old daughter could only go so fast. She was fairly tired out from their trek already. They had now gone about one mile with the bear following them, and it had gotten to within about fifty feet of them. There was no mistaking that it was following them. The father turned to face the bear, and it stopped. He picked up a rock and threw it back at the bear, but the bear did not move.

Then the trio of hikers turned and walked as fast as they could away from the bear. It started out behind them as soon as they took off. After a hundred yards, the father turned to face the bear again. It stopped immediately, but it had gained another five feet on them! The parents were becoming frantic now. They picked up some rocks and threw them at the bear again. The bear did not retreat. The father took the pink fanny pack from his daughter and picked her up.

This time when the hikers turned to leave, they decided they were not going to turn around again, but just keep on going as fast as they could. They covered several hundred yards, but the father just had to look and see where that bear was. It was right behind them about 30 feet back. The trio stopped, and the father placed himself between the bear and his family. The bear once again had stopped and was simply watching them. Father yelled, but the bear did not budge.

Now the hikers took off again with father carrying the little girl. This time they kept an eye on the bear. It followed and still kept gaining on them. When they stopped for a moment and faced the bear, it stopped. When they turned to leave, it followed. When it was getting down to within the last twenty feet, there were several stops with frantic parents yelling at the crazy bear. They just could not imagine why this was all happening. They were afraid that the bear was after their daughter.

Things were really getting tense now. The bear was within about ten feet. There was more stopping than there was retreating. The couple yelled and waved their arms, but the bear just stood and watched them. Then it stepped towards them when they were not even moving away. The couple holding their daughter backed away. The bear advanced, the couple retreated backwards down the roadbed.

Finally, as a last resort, when the bear was just a few feet away, the father took the pink fanny pack and threw it out in the woods behind the bear. Immediately the bear turned and ran after the fanny pack just like a dog after a stick.

The hikers turned and fled back to their vehicle at the parking area which was about a quarter mile away. The bear did not follow them. The hikers reported this incident, and the father requested help in retrieving the pink fanny pack. Ranger Pete Kemppainen returned to the area with the father to search for it.

Since the spot where the pink fanny pack was tossed was easy to locate, the search for it later that afternoon was successful. It turns out that the father had a wallet containing about $375 in the pack which he naturally did not want to lose. That was recovered. The bright pink fanny pack, which the daughter loved so much to wear, also contained a HAM SANDWICH. The ham sandwich was not recovered.

And thus ended another bear (or should we say people) incident in the Porkies.

BEARFALL

A large bear was sighted coming somewhat towards the campers, who were from Baltimore. The bear paid no attention to them, though. It just walked right through their camp, right past them as they sat next to their fire and headed straight for where they had hung - you guessed it - the food. This was a couple hundred feet from camp. It was about a half hour after sunset, so the campers could still see the bear fairly well.

It climbed right up the food stash tree and batted at the hanging food bag with a paw. The food bag swung away, but when it swung back the bear grabbed for it. The bear fell out of the tree twice before he got the food bag.

The next day, the campers followed the bear's tracks. They estimated that the bear weighed between three and four hundred pounds. They were able to locate the remains of their food bag along with the remains of someone else's food bag who had apparently had the same experience with the bear previously.

1995

It was expected that there would be numerous early bear problems at the Porkies in 1995 after the record breaking number the previous year. This did not happen, however. Most of the 1995 problems centered around the Carp Rivermouths, Presque Isle and the Mirror Lake areas and were mostly due to two large sows with cubs. One of these raided in the Mirror Lake area, the other was hitting both of the Carp Rivermouths and Presque Isle.

The bear pole materials for the interior campsites were received in mid summer. The bear proof trash containers arrived late in October. They will be installed starting in 1996. Now, here are some of the 1995 stories.

WHEN THE STROLLS OF NOVEMBEAR COME EARLY

The last full week of February, 1995 was quite wintery. Highs were never above the twenties, and the lows were in the single digits above zero to well below zero on most of the nights. It was very cold and windy. Not exactly the right time of year for a bear story, right? On approximately February 25th, I registered a young man who was going winter backpacking alone. After taking care of the paperwork for his permit and asking a list of questions which Porkies rangers always ask winter campers, he asked me if there would be any bear problems.

This question sort of startled me because it was winter and a very cold part of winter at that. Since no backpacker had asked me that question for at least four months previously, I did not have a ready answer and had to think about his question for a bit. My answer was: "Well its winter, and the bears hibernate during the winter. There shouldn't be any out at this time of year. They normally will be in their dens until April when it gets a lot warmer. Once in awhile they will come out earlier for a short time during warm spells. This is one of the coldest periods of this winter, and I sincerely doubt you will have any problem with or see any bears. It would be a good idea to hang your food anyway, because there are other animals around which would be happy to get into it for you."

Off went the backpacker to go camp. Back to selling downhill ski tow tickets went I. Within a day, one of the Porkies other rangers reported the sighting of a small cub bear near the Whitetail cabin. I suspected that someone was mistaken. I was wrong. The next day, two of the ski hill rangers, Ken Marlow and Roy Pederson, reported they had seen a small cub bear running around in the old Union Bay service area. Considering the extremely cold weather, this seemed very unlikely, but enough rangers had seen the little cub by now that we were sure it was out of its den wandering around.

Within a few more days, several other reports of the small cub bear came in from various locations around Union Bay. First in the old Service Area, then at the picnic sites along Lake Superior, then Don Harris saw it in Silver City.

Each sighting of the cub was further to the east. At least the backpacker I had talked to had headed to the west. He was not going to see Novembear, which is the name I have given to our cold winter traveling cub. Novembear was next sighted near Green, which is halfway to Ontonagon from the Porkies. Finally, Novembear's winter wanderings came to an end, but not on a bad note.

Novembear was sighted by Joe Gehl, Jr. of Ontonagon. His parents operate the Sunshine Motel. Joe saw the cub and followed it until it went up into a tree near Dreiss Creek. He then contacted the Ontonagon County Sheriff's Department. Sheriff Kitzman and Deputy Lorendo responded. Deputy Lorendo apparently grabbed the bear, not without some damage to his clothing, and placed it into a container.

The cub was turned over to Baraga Department of Natural Resources personnel. They planned to radio collar the cub, reintroduce the cub into an open den and follow its movements to make sure it successfully returns to the wild. Thus ended Novembear's midwinter trek heading east toward the Mighty Mac.

FOOD HANGING METHODS FOR CABIN USERS?

For some reason several of the groups renting park cabins this summer decided to hang their food outside in the tree branches rather than keep it inside of their cabin units.

According to Paula Simmons, one of the Porkies' Summer Rangers, the Hansen party lost their food at the Section 17 Cabin the night of June 23, 1995. They hung their food in their backpack outside in a tree. When reporting this, they were advised that first, it is not proper to hang food in a pack, unless one does not value the pack very much. Second, if one is renting a cabin, it is neither necessary nor desirable to hang food outside of the cabin. It is not necessary because the cabin is available to keep the food in. Only backpackers who must sleep in a tent or on the ground in a sleeping bag and have no other way to keep their food away from bears need to hang it up. It is not desirable because the bears will take the food if they can get it, as they did in this case.

On July 7th, Ranger Mike Rafferty reported that the Day party put their food outside at the Little Carp River Cabin. Once again, the food was hung outside in one of the cabin users' backpacks. They did this to keep the mice which infested that cabin from getting into it. That would qualify as a fairly big mistake.

There are ways to mouseproof the food inside of the cabin. It is easier to mouseproof than it is to hunt the next day for the lost pack which contained the driver's license and a good knife, none of which were ever found. The bear probably did not eat the knife, but he might very well have eaten the drivers license. It probably depends on how good it smelled.

MIDNIGHT MADNESS

The three backpackers in the Talarico party selected the Little Carp Rivermouth campsite for their evening stay. Being used to backpacking in the Rockies, the Porkies by comparison seemed pretty tame elevation wise. However, the Porkies can produce first class all American bear experiences as the party discovered around midnight.

First, a lone bear ambled into camp and rooted around at the base of a tree. A few minutes later, another bear wandered into the opposite side of camp. The campers remained very quiet listening and waiting to discover what this chance meeting between the two bruins would produce. The second of the two bears now brushed against one of the backpacker's tents startling the occupant. Then there was nothing but breathless silence again for a moment.

Suddenly there was an extensive series of loud grunts, snarls and squeals. Then total silence again. Eventually the packers went to sleep. At dawn, the three packers awoke to find the score left by the participants in the previous night's bear dispute. This may well have been produced on a previous occasion.

The score was clearly left on a heavily marked tree. One bear had apparently left heavy claw scrapings six feet high on the tree trunk. The other bear, which was considerably larger, left extensive and heavy claw marks ten feet high on the trunk. It seems pretty obvious which of the two bruins won this round of nonviolent one upbearship.

The Rockies veterans were quite excited by their bear encounter, even though they did not actually see the bears. They did take pictures of the marked up tree trunk to remind them of their spine tingling incident in the future.

LOSING YOUR BEARINGS IN PORCUPINE MOUNTAINS

In midsummer 1995, two lady backpackers reported to Ranger Tony Sassin that someone had stolen their food cache a couple nights previously. Tony suggested that a bear had probably gotten their hung food stash, but the ladies insisted that it was no bear which got the food. Their food had been STOLEN by SOMEONE.

Tony once again pointed out that many backpackers lose their food to bears in the Porkies. There are bears which specialize in separating packers and their food supplies. Still, the ladies were insistent that no bear was involved. The rope had been cleanly cut off, probably by a knife wielding person. They had heard someone giggling out in the woods at one time. No, most assuredly it was no bear which could have taken their food, it had been stolen by a person.

Tony asked the ladies if they had seen anyone. They replied that it was much too dark to see anything when this had happened. Tony, sort of surprised, pointed out that it would be impossible for anyone to have been wandering around stealing food bags of backpackers if it was completely pitch black out. The ladies seemed to be prepared with a ready answer for Tony's suggestion. The thief must have had night vision goggles!

At this, Tony finally gave up trying to convince the ladies that it was undoubtedly a bear which had taken their food. Even if the rope was snipped off cleanly, a bear could easily have done that. Bears come naturally equipped with sharp instruments. As for the giggling, a state park does have people in it, and sometimes they do giggle. That is certainly no evidence that a person stole their food. Tony is a professional and did not mention these facts. It is not a ranger's job to argue with people who believe that they have had their food stolen from them. Instead, he filled out an incident report indicating that the ladies had reported their food stolen.

A similar report was made that summer by a man who had his pack taken in the middle of the night. That camper also insisted that the missing pack had been stolen. He even claimed that when he went outside of his tent after hearing noise, he saw a person running away in the dark. When his pack was found, it was very clear that no one had stolen it, but that an animal had taken it for some goodies or smell it contained. His cellular phone was still inside of it.

Why was it that this summer there were people who insisted that other people had taken their food rather than accepting the most likely, most logical and most obvious reason - that the ever present bears which specialize in this activity had done it? There was a reason for this which became more clear later.

Several days after the two ladies reported the theft of their food, I happened to be in the Porkies Visitor Center and overheard a male cabin user telling the store clerk about two lady backpackers he and his wife had met on the trail. It turns out that this couple had gone to the Mirror Lake 2 bunk cabin, and had met the two lady backpackers on the way in. The ladies had no food because someone had stolen it according to them. The couple in the store had given some of their food to the ladies.

At this point in his story, the man's wife interrupted him and told him to tell us the rest of it - about the two ladies. The guy sort of chuckled and said that the ladies claimed that the Michigan Militia must have been on night maneuvers in Porcupine Mountains State Park. They were able to do this at night because they were equipped with night vision goggles. It was someone from the Michigan Militia who had stolen their food.

Now, to put this story in its proper perspective, remember that the bombing of the Federal Building in Oklahoma City had occurred in April of 1995. For a considerable period of time following that terrible tragedy, the major media in the United States continually broadcast all kinds of completely unsupported allegations concerning the Michigan Militia's involvement in the bombing.

The two lady backpackers in Porcupine Mountains State Park were merely applying to their current surroundings their understanding of reality as shaped by our media. They were from a major metropolitan area, possibly in California. Here they were in Michigan where that terrible Michigan Militia was located. Everyone knows (in the summer of 1995) that the Michigan Militia were somehow or other connected with or remotely responsible in some way for everything which is bad, from bad breath to missing food.

Does the media really have that much influence on people's understanding of reality? I think that they do. It's quite frightening actually. Well, lets go with the flow. Here's my version of the ladies' story through their eyes with my twist. The following story is FICTION.

THE BLACK BEARETS AND THE MICHIGAN MILITIA

Last night, the elite Black Bearet Unit suspected to be part of the Michigan Militia conducted night maneuvers in the vast Porcupine Mountains Wilderness State Park according to anonymous sources. After conducting reconnaissance throughout the Park, they carried out their main assignments with considerable skill and ease - they located and took the food stashes of various Porkies backpacking campers. With one or two exceptions, the backpackers were not even aware that the Black Bearets were nearby conducting their surveillance. In almost every instance, the Black Bearets are able to snitch the packers food and leave their victims with the impression that a black bear took it.

These night raids in the Porkies are believed to be the main source of food supplies for the Black Bearet Unit and possibly the rest of the Michigan Militia as well. They also help supply it with a wide assortment of camping knives, hatchets, stoves, water bottles, packs (lots of packs), as well as an occasional false ID or cellular phone. It is also believed that the Black Bearets are practicing night maneuvers in the Porcupine Mountains in preparation for seizing that important strategic area in order to take everything from the backpackers.

The Black Bearet Unit has trained so well at its food snitching task that even the Porkies Rangers are regularly deceived into thinking that black bears are actually responsible for the massive food losses by Park backpackers. What a silly idea. The problem has become so great that sources indicate several Michigan legislators are considering laws to punish anyone who claims to be a Black Bearet or who imitates a bear in any way.

REALITY BITES

By now most people have probably seen the cellular phone advertisement on television where the bear is tearing up a backpacking camp, while the male member of the camping party frantically reaches out of his tent for his cellular phone. At last, the phone is reached. It had been conveniently placed outside the tent on a log. Yeah, right! Presumably the camper then calls for help from the Rangers so they can save he and his wife from the marauding bruin.

First of all, think about this scenario. What are the Rangers, who are probably miles away by foot trails, supposed to do? Maybe the camper can hold up the phone and a Ranger can yell at the bear over it. I'm sure the camper could yell louder than that himself. Then again, maybe the camper is sending in a last known location report that the Rangers can follow up on later? Let me tell you, the television version of this type of incident is not at all what really happens out in the woods.

But before we get into that, be aware that some campers have actually found useful purposes for cellular phones. One time a lost camper called the old Porcupine Mountains State Park Headquarters on a cellular phone to find out where he was. This occurred in late April. It turned out that he was parked at the Porkies Visitor Center gate which was closed and locked. It was so early in the season that the signs indicating locations and directions had not yet been installed. [They were installed very quickly thereafter.]

On another occasion in midsummer 1995, a family party heading to one of the Mirror Lake cabins for a week's stay in Porcupine Mountains used a cellular phone to call the Park Headquarters to report that they were stranded. They were heading three miles in by foot trail and were taking a canoe with them. In preparation they had placed the canoe on one of those carriers which rolls the canoe along on a bicycle wheel. Then they had placed all of their gear into the canoe to try and roll it three miles over the rugged trails to their cabin. Since they had no backpacking type gear, but only regular sized stove, coolers, sleeping bags, etc., the single bicycle wheel had collapsed unexpectedly and completely without warning under the several hundred pounds of weight.

The cabin users then used their cellular phone to summon a Ranger to see if he knew how to get the gear into Mirror Lake for them somehow. By the way, this party had only made it about one hundred yards before the wheel had collapsed. They still had about 2.9 miles to go. Other than to carry the gear in by several round trips, the Ranger had no idea how to get that much gear into the Mirror Lake Cabin area. He suggested that they get a cabin closer to the road next time.

Well, enough of that, back to the cellular phone bear incident. There was a lady backpacker who lost her pack to a bear in 1995. This was in the Big Carp Rivermouth area. She searched the area the following day for her missing backpack. She was never able to find it. However, she did manage to locate a backpack which someone else had lost to a bear. It was the pack which a man had reported stolen by a person on the interior of the Park.

While inspecting the lost pack which she had found, she discovered a cellular phone inside. Now this is a lot more like what actually happens out in the woods in backpacking country than what was depicted in the TV commercial regarding cellular phones. The chances of the backpacker actually being able to put a cellular phone to some useful purpose are slim. Packers put the really important things, like cellular phones and keys for their transportation, inside their packs, then put their food in there, and hang the whole thing up as if it were in an office safe.

My father once told me that when I got older it would become clear to me that people were strange, and that the older I got, the more strange people would seem. He was right about this. No self respecting backpacker would want a cellular phone inside of his tent. First of all, they went backpacking to get away from it all, so why would they want a phone right in the tent with them? I don't know, that's why I'm asking you.

Besides, if they had a phone in the tent, they might be subjected to crank, obscene or sale's pitch phone calls during their vacation. Leaving the phone laying outside of the tent on a log is the stuff of TV fiction. It might get wet out there, or a bear might make a long distance call to some Panda in northern China and charge it to them. No, packers are much more likely to hang their things with the food. There is no way they could really dial 911 to get a Lone Ranger to yell at the bear for them when they need it, and the above real life case proves it.

DESPERADO AND THE THREE AMIGOS

As noted in the introduction for 1995, the main problem this year was with two different large sows with cubs. The worst of these was dubbed Desperado and the Three Amigos by Summer Ranger Angela Nelson. This quartet mainly raided the Big and Little Carp Rivermouth backpack campgrounds and the Presque Isle campground. Desperado was estimated to weigh around 250 pounds, and the Amigos about 30 pounds each.

THE BEST LAID PLANS OF BEARS AND MEN

On August 2, 1995, Desperado and the Three Amigos started a camp raid which they could not finish. Angela Nelson reported that the Pickler party had a run in with the marauding quartet. It was fairly uneventful because the Pickler's dog immediately treed the Amigos. Desperado lurked around camp for a long time and eventually took up a post at the base of the tree the Amigos were in. She apparently did not leave this spot until dawn when the cubs finally came down.

However, a different bear did cause the Picklers some grief. A yearling bear raided their camp throughout the night. First, it got a pack with food inside, but the campers managed to retrieve the pack after the bear got the food. Everyone went to bed. Later, at 4:30 AM, the yearling returned to try for the other pack which was hung with the rest of the food inside. This one had Kool-Aid inside - yummy! The bear climbed the food hanging tree, ripped open the pack, bent the pack's bars and feasted on the sausage and jerky inside.

Once again the pack was retrieved, but this one seemed to have been damaged a little. Again we remind everyone not to hang food in your pack unless you are trying new and unique ways to force yourself to buy a new one.

SOCIAL CLIMBING IN THE PORKIES

After the early disappointing showing in the above incident, Desperado started to teach the Amigos to climb the food bag trees and get food bags, according to Angela. Of course, in most of their raiding situations the fearsome foursome did not have to worry about the Pickler party's dog. This left Desperado free to have the little rascals do the climbing wherever they wanted and without unwanted interference.

On August 16th, the quarrelsome quartet showed up at the Erbes camp near Explorers Falls on the Little Carp River. The cubs went up after the food bags and then fought over the syrup, butter, raisins, apple sauce, trail mix and Kool-Aid. There was a jar of Jif peanut butter which is still missing. As noted in one of the Copper Harbor stories, choosy bears apparently do choose Jif.

The campers decided to bang pots and pans together. This time it worked, scaring the bears away, at least temporarily. The campers had a good supply of canned goods which the Amigos were unable to gain entry to apparently. All of the cans were recovered. All were dented and slobbered on.

TECHNICAL CLIMBING IN THE PORKIES

Over time, Desperado and the Three Amigos improved their food snatching skills quite a bit. The Amigos even learned a method to shimmy up the "bear proof" food hanging poles which the Rangers had installed to prevent bears from getting backpackers' food supplies.

On August 29th, the Johnson party from Ypsilanti witnessed the bear pole caper. When one of the Amigos went up the bear pole, the campers yelled at the bears. Then the Amigos all came over to the campers' tents. Then the Amigos headed back to the bear pole, and up one went again. Then the campers yelled again, and the Amigos headed over to the tents again. This situation repeated itself numerous times just like a stuck record. According to Sandy Richardson, the Park Receptionist, the Johnson party got very little if any sleep that night.

THE PRESQUE ISLE RAIDS

There were a couple of noteworthy bear happenings at the Presque Isle Campground in 1995. These were undoubtedly caused by Desperado and the Three Amigos. According to Presque Isle Head Ranger Dave Braithwaite, the Three Amigos got in the habit of tearing up screen tents just to go in and look around. This did not endear them too much with the Presque Isle campers who had screen tents.

In the first of the Presque Isle incidents we will describe, there was tent damage, and in the second, damage to a tent trailer. Not all of the damage was necessarily caused by the bears.

The first incident occurred at one of the campsites on the west end of the campground along the bluff overlooking the Lake Superior shoreline. After dark, a bear or bears, entered the site and started tearing up things in the screen tent which was closer to the road. Although the campers did not know it, because they did not try to look, this was probably the Three Amigos doing their screen tent thing. The camping party was in a tent, and the door of the tent opened toward the road and screen tent. The campers became upset by all of the noise and decided to get out of there, but they were not going to go out the door of the tent towards the noisy bears.

So, one camper made a decision. He took a knife and made a long slice down the back of their tent. Then the campers slipped out through the slit and quietly clambered over the bank and down the hillside part way towards Lake Superior. This is steep and rough terrain. They then threaded their way east through the towering virgin timber towards the lake access stairway. When they reached the stairway, they ascended back up into the campground.

Here, they had to decide where to go. Their car was on their campsite far to the west end of the campground, but the bears were there tearing up their screen tent in which they must have left their cooler or something. They were not going to go there. The toilet building was also to the west, but it was only half way across the campground. Warily, they headed towards the toilet building, which was back in the direction of their campsite, hoping all the way that the bear or bears were still back on their site destroying things in their screen tent. They reached the toilet building without incident. Then they spent a most uncomfortable night in the toilet building, waiting until sunup before returning to camp to assess the previous night's damage.

As far as I know, the only real damage to the camp, other than some slight damage to their screen tent, was a large knife slash down the back of their tent.

The other Presque Isle incident involved campers staying in a tent trailer. There were a number of nearby camps with relatives who were in the area for a wedding. During the night, za bear came to the tent trailer. It was probably Desperado. She apparently smelled food. Usually, black bears do not bother tent trailers. However, this tendency can be overcome by campers if they are sloppy with their food, garbage or food odors. There was food in the tent trailer's refrigerator. I suspect there were fairly strong food odors present.

In any event, the bear went up to the trailer in the middle of the night near the front passenger side corner. One of the Lance party from Greenwood, South Carolina was sleeping on that corner just inside. The bear glommed onto the corner with its mouth and paws and proceeded to shake the entire trailer. The camper woke up and thought his brother, sleeping in a van nearby, was playing a practical joke. He yelled at his brother a couple of times. His brother woke up and with eveybody yelling, the bear was scared away.

The tent trailer had large tears in the front, and fabric was torn from the roof also. Remember, all you folks who use tent trailers, your campers are half trailer; but they are also half tent. You should take the same types of precautions which tent users take. If you have food storage areas inside your tent trailer, you must keep it very clean and free from odors.

IF THE SHOE FITS

Bob Schue of Minneapolis had a most distressing bear and racoon incident at the Union Bay Campground late in 1995. In fact, this is the last bear incident recorded for that year. Bob was tenting with his children on the east end of the campground along the Lake Superior shoreline.

On the night of October 20, there was a major storm on the lake. In fact, the largest waves I have ever seen at Union Bay were present around 9 AM on October 21. It should be noted here that there have been bigger waves, but they usually occur at night and are therefore not actually witnessed.

Anyway, I noticed upon entering the campground that the waves were washing across the lower campground road in places and that a large log was being pushed up against one of the camps in the middle of the campground. I immediately started waking up campers along the lake and advising them to move to higher ground. Bob's camp was contacted last because it was protected somewhat by trees and shrubs from direct hits of wave washed debris.

After everyone else got away from the lakeshore, I returned to Bob's camp. It was then that the previous night's animal shenanigans came to light. Bob had placed a plastic bag full of garbage on top of his relatively new 4-wheel drive vehicle.

During the night, a bear had come and torn up the garbage. It also pried at the vent windows on the vehicle and managed to force the one on the driver's side open. Apparently, it then reached inside and grasped some food items to remove.

Later, racoons entered the vehicle through the open window. It was the racoons which caused the worst of the mess. There was a half gallon of milk spilled on the front passenger floor. The food within the vehicle was all messed up, torn apart, chewed on and spread around. There were racoon scats at several places on top of the camping gear which was heaped inside the vehicle.

The Rangers always recommend that food smells be kept to a bare minimum at campsites. This means that all garbage should be removed from the campsite and placed into the garbage dumpsters provided near the campground office. For those who insist on keeping garbage at their campsite, the usual result is a mess to clean up in the morning. Sometimes the mess is a small one. Bob's mess was a big one. He decided not to stay longer, cleaned up the mess and headed back home.

But even though the Schues had a bad experience with the animals, they still had a good outdoor experience overall. They learned that the bears and racoons actually do come around the campsites during the night, and they got to see the raw power of a major Lake Superior storm firsthand. The noise from the crashing of the waves near their camp was numbing, and the waves were truly a sight to behold.

BRAVEHEART

There was one interior camp where the camper involved would not let the Mirror Lake area bully bear get into the camp. This story is last because the exact year has been forgotten, as well as the hardy camperette's name. She stopped at the Visitor Center and informed me that a large bear had attempted to get her and her partner's food as they were preparing to depart from Mirror Lake. They were camped on a small hilltop just east of the Mirror Lake 8 Bunk Cabin.

The bear came from the north and tried to walk into the campsite. Yelling and waving her arms, the young lady met the bear would not let it pass her. The bear retreated into the woods. Shortly thereafter, the bear appeared again coming from the west and tried again to enter the campsite. Once again, yelling and waving her arms, the lady ran and confronted the bear. The bruin retreated again, but not for long.

This scenario was repeated several more times with the bear trying to sneak in from other directions. Trying to enter the camp about six times, the bear made a complete circle around the camp on the little hill. Every time, the young woman went where many would not dare to tread and met the bear head on. The camping couple managed to pack all of their gear, including all of their food, and leave without other incident. I gave the young lady deserved praise.

Not many backpackers take anywhere near enough precautions with their food. In many cases, backpackers actually give food to bears thinking that they are somehow exchanging it for their own personal safety. There was an incident of this sort along the Little Carp River during one of the last four years. A small group of backpackers saw a bear off in the distance on the other side of the river. In order to save their food supply, they felt it was necessary to throw some of their food across the river towards the bear. I guess this was sort of like an offering or something. When they started this activity, the bear was more than 100 feet away and not paying any attention to them. Their tossing food across the river seemed to be the only reason the bear altered its course and headed towards them.

THE OUTLOOK FOR 1996
A RISING BEAROMETER?

The winter of 1995-1996 was very severe with record snowfall in some areas and near records in others. The temperatures were cold and the spring temperatures have been well below average. The bear in this area normally come out of hibernation during late March or early April. This year there was still from one to four feet of snow on the ground in the Porkies during that period of time. In areas near deer yards, there was a large amount of carrion in the woods for the bear to eat this year due to widespread starvation of the deer. In other areas, there was practically nothing for the emerging bears to eat out in the woods.

So what are the hungry bears doing to get food? Well, we know what two of them have been doing.

THE BEAR MALL REVISITED

One of the area bruins has already appeared at The Bear Mall during a raid on the Konteka Restaurant's bird feeding stations. This occurred at the White Pine Mall on April 29th as reported in the *Ironwood Daily Globe*. The bear ate all the bird feed and suet and destroyed a separate bird feeder and ate all the bird food and suet outside the Konteka Restaurant's large viewing windows. John Razmus, operator of the Konteka, said that this bear was very hungry. There is a high probability that this bear was one of those which regularly visited the Konteka last summer.

STRAIGHT ARROW

Observations on the second bruin come from long time Porkies employee and trapper, Dave Peloso. These observations consist entirely of reconstructions of what the bear did from its tracks left in the snow. Dave indicated that in his decades of trapping he has never witnessed this type of behavior before. He considers it very much out of the ordinary for a bear. This occurred during the first week of April when there was still two feet or more of snow on the ground in the area.

While heading out to inspect a beaver pond, Dave noticed bear tracks. He also noticed that they were not just meandering around as bear tracks usually do. Instead, these were going in a straight line and generally in the same direction he was traveling. When Dave arrived at the beaver pond, he discovered that it was the destination of the bear as well as himself. While he never saw this bear, its activities were plainly evident from its tracks and the damage it left behind at the beaver pond.

The bear had attempted to tear up the beaver lodge. It was not successful because the pond was still well frozen. This bear managed to dig a hole in the top and on the side of the lodge but was not able to tear the lodge apart. The bear had also sought out the various feeding stations where beavers store food underground around the pond for the winter. It was able to dig these up, but there was no evidence the bear got any of the beavers.

The tracks indicated that the bear had gone all around the pond, sniffing out each spot where the beavers spent their time. The bear went out on the dam where there was some open water. This water coming out of the pond has the smell of the resident beavers and their waste. A bear can probably pick up such a scent from a considerable distance away. The bear's tracks left this pond, and once again, they went in a straight line off into the woods.

Dave really did not want to meet this obviously very hungry bear. He also decided not to trap at this pond because the bear would probably take anything he caught and might very well damage his equipment. Also, there might be a run in with the bruin at some future time. This, Dave sincerely wished to avoid. So, he moved on to the next pond which he wished to inspect for possible trapping.

Well, you can probably guess what he found upon arrival there. Bear tracks came straight out of the woods with a repeat of the tracks and damage to beaver things which had occurred at the previous pond. The tracks and damage indicated that the bear attempted to tear apart the lodge, tore up feeding stations all around the pond, went out on the dam, and left the pond going in a straight line again. Undoubtedly, it had headed off directly to another beaver pond.

Dave decided it was definitely time to head off, in a different direction this time. According to him, all indications were that the bear was extremely hungry, was unsuccessful at getting any beaver so far, and was probably very frustrated. Taken together and applied to a large bear, this results in a dangerous situation for beavers and people who trap them.

The bears in many areas of the Upper Peninsula are going to be in a predicament very similar to the above bear until the unusually heavy snow cover melts off. As of May 10th, there is still a lot of snow in the higher elevations of Porcupine Mountains and elsewhere in the Copper Country. Time will tell how the bears will be affected by the severe winter.

THE END OF THE TALES

In this section there are several stories from various years.

LEAVING PORCUPINE MOUNTAINS

There are a few more details available regarding the September 4th, 1992, incident which occurred to Ken Shaw and his friend as described in *The Last of the Bear Raids* on page 126. As noted there, it was apparently Schizo The Wonder Bear who raided their camp and took everything.

The incident took place around 8:30 PM. Ranger Rick Tessmer, while on patrol later that night, found the two men sleeping in the Lake of the Clouds parking lot. One was sleeping under their car, and the other was sleeping on the stone wall beside the parking lot. These do not sound like particularly comfortable places for sleep to me. The reason they were not sleeping in their vehicle is they lost their car keys to the bear when it took everything. The keys had been in their pack.

Rick described the method which the bear used to separate the backpackers from their gear. The bear came around the camp where the two men had a fire. Fire did not deter the bear at all. This bear could not be spooked. The men apparently picked up their pack and then put it down away from the bear, which entered their campsite and started towards the pack. The two backpackers stood between the bear and the pack facing the bear.

Since this incident started just as it got dark, the campers got out their lighting gear - one penlight sized flashlight. The bear went to the left to go around the campers, and they went to the left to block it. Then the bruin went to the right. They went to the right. Then the bear went back to the left, which the campers countered with the same move. This little zigzag dance occurred numerous times until somehow the bear was at the pack, and the campers were on the edge of the woods away from it. The campers, as could be expected, had paid a lot more attention to where the bear was than to where the pack was. It's hard to know exactly where that pack is when you're watching the bear so closely.

These guys were having such great luck that it was bound to continue - and it did. Just as the bear got what it was after, the battery in the penlight gave out. Since it was now quite dark, the two backpackers decided it would be best to abandon all of their gear to the bear. They left their camp on the south side of the bridge below Lake of the Clouds Overlook and went up to the scenic area parking lot where their car was located. Being locked out of it, they then went to sleep on the ground.

When Ranger Rick found them much later, he took pity upon them and offered to loan them a tent to sleep in for the night. They willingly accepted his offer. I assume that they were able to locate their car keys when they retrieved their damaged gear the next day. Mr. Shaw returned the park's tent on the 5th and got a refund for the next three nights on which they had planned to camp. The bear got four days worth of food. Not a bad fifteen minutes' worth of work for the bear, eh?

FLIRTING WITH DISASTER

This is an old story from 1977, which just has never been told yet. It was remembered by Park Rangers Marty Williamson and Don Harris. I had forgotten all about it. The incident occurred to Don Harris while working at the Presque Isle area. Don was collecting trash at the Presque Isle campground in an old International pickup truck. The trash was in plastic bags and was simply tossed into the truck for later hauling to the dump.

There had been a bear hanging around the day use area at Presque Isle for some time. Back in 1977, there was a loop drive around the no longer existing park office, which was located near the top of the lower waterfalls stairway. It was at the old office where this incident happened. Today, this is the open area which one walks through to get to the falls when coming from the overnight parking lot at Presque Isle.

Don pulled into the area and drove right up next to the open porch of the office building. The International's passenger side door was right next to the porch on the corner of the building. As Don rolled to a stop, the bear came trotting up and started to climb up into the bed of the truck on Don's side. As Don was getting out, the bruin popped its mouth at Don, who had not noticed the bear behind him. Don shut the door and stayed in the truck for a moment. Then, realizing he had no exit on his side of the truck, Don slid across the seat and exited the passenger door to the porch. He took two quick steps across the porch to the office door, opened the screen and tried to enter. The door was locked! He pounded on the door and yelled for the ranger who lived in the back to unlock the door.

Meanwhile, the bear had climbed up into the truck bed and was spitting and popping its mouth at Don, who was only about ten feet away from it. Don squeezed between the screen door and the locked entrance door trying to shut the screen like he was not even there (as if that would somehow protect him from the unfriendly bruin.) After a few more bangs on the door and yells, Don realized that he should be very quiet and still so as not to upset the bear further. The screen door at least gave him some sense of security - there was something between him and the bear. So Don resisted his urge to bang and yell. Instead, he remained quiet and motionless for the eternity it took for the door to be unlocked by the Ranger who lived in the back of the office. This was actually only about one minute. However, remember that time is relative.

This bear always seemed to display a fairly nasty temper. It had mange, was quite skinny and had a very large belly. Don thought it also had worms or was sick in some way. Once this bear found garbage in a truck, the garbage belonged to it, and it would not tolerate people approaching. Even though Don brought the garbage to this spot, the bear considered him as a threat to its garbage supply.

A few days later, another employee of the Park was in the office when the same bear got in the garbage truck. This employee was not very familiar with this bear. He grabbed his camera, opened the door, and went out the screen door to take a picture. The bear turned to meet him, greeting him with the standard unpleasant spitting, huffing and popping of the mouth. The employee retreated back into the office immediately. He then tried to sneak out just enough to get one picture. He succeeded.

It took a special effort to trap this bear. Apparently, it had been trapped before and just would not enter the trap. Finally, Don gave it the raspberry. He obtained some raspberry preserves to bait the trap with. Don said the bear could not resist them. The bruin went around and around the trap looking inside. It kept this up for a considerable time, and finally, in it went. Unfortunately, this bear had to be destroyed.

THE LITTLE RASCALS

There were a couple of interesting observations of bear cubs by Park personnel in 1992. Summer Ranger Paula Simmons saw a bear cub chase a fawn around the Lake of the Clouds permit booth two times on June 16th. The chase apparently ended when the fawn's mother showed up.

Three days later, a Summer Ranger saw three small cubs ahead of him on the side of the road. He stopped the pickup truck he was driving fairly close to the little bruins. One ran across in front of him. The other two took the scenic route and went under his truck. He could not tell for sure if the two which went under actually came out on the other side or if they were still under the truck. They were still under there playing around. In fact, as I recall, the other one came back and joined those two playing all around the truck. The Ranger had to wait awhile and finally blow the horn to get the little rascals on their way again.

FLASHBACKS

Remember *The Copper Harbor Taste Test* (see page 74) in which teenagers took a smallish car belonging to their parents and put two different brands of peanut butter on either side of the hood and front fenders to see which one the bears at the Copper Harbor dump would prefer? I just thought it would be nice to let everyone know that there was a very similar occurrence back at that period of time involving honey placed on a car at the Copper Harbor dump. Many of the circumstances of this honey on the car incident were almost identical to the peanut butter incident except they were different teens and were not trying to compare different brands utilizing the bears. They were just plain trying to attract the bruins. This incident also involved their parents' vehicle and resulted in some slight damage to the car, which the teens tried to conceal as best they could. This was a different batch of teens and a different vehicle, however.

A few years ago in midsummer, a bear which weighed about 125 pounds came wandering around the permit booth at Lake of the Clouds Scenic Area. The occupant of the booth, one of the Summer Rangers, was not particularly at ease when the bruin passed between the booth and the pop cooler just outside of the booth door. The bear was just exploring its territory and was not trying to upset the booth attendant, in spite of what the booth attendant might have thought.

EPILOGUE

There is hope that bear/human confrontations of the type described in this book can be greatly reduced, if not entirely eliminated. It is going to take a major educational campaign to do so, as the stories above indicate. Now that Porcupine Mountains Wilderness State Park will be starting to install bear proof trash containers and more bear poles for backpackers, the horrific food losses by the campers to bears should be reduced.

There are new developments in bear repellent and avoidance technology, which can help alleviate bear problems. The new bear proof food cannisters which are designed for backpackers are one of these. They are fairly small containers in which food is always carried and stored. Bears are unable to open them; and when they try, the worst which usually happens is that the cannister has to be located after the bear swats it away into the underbrush. As for repellents, the pepper sprays usually do well for making bears prefer to be elsewhere.

In November of 1996, there may be a proposal on the general election ballot in Michigan, which would ban the use of dogs or bait for bear hunting in the state. Anyone who is familiar with bears, bear habits, bear numbers, or bear hunting will quickly realize that such a proposal, if passed, may have detrimental consequences which are entirely unforeseen by those who vote for it. Bear overpopulation is one possibility. Overpopulation can lead to widespread starvation during severe winters, a situation all too evident this past winter for the deer population. Another possibility, which the author considers a probability, is even more bear problems for campers and those who live in bear country.

Those who are against a ban on use of bait point out that it is much safer to have the bear come to the hunter, who does not have to wander all over in the forest looking for the bear. The hunter establishes a bait in an area where he has clear sight of what is approaching the bait. Guess which type of bear is more likely to go to a hunter's bait - one which always avoids people or one which searches them out to take their food? While the author is not and has never been a bear hunter, he does not favor the proposed ban. It is just another attempt by a small committed group to utilize the government to stop an activity which they do not like. A problem here is that bans always lead to evasions of the bans.

If there are actually more bear problems after such a ban, the likely consequence will be that Rangers have to destroy more problem bears in the summer, a task we do not relish. Also, homeowners in the more remote areas of the state are going to have to put up with more bear problems and damage, or hope that the government can solve the problems for them. If the government cannot solve the problems, the property owners will.

The bear population, at least until the winter of '95-'96, was doing very well. The need for a ban of the type proposed is not at all clear to me. Once again, I suspect it is more of an anti-hunting thing.

What almost everyone would like with respect to Michigan's black bears is a good, healthy, stable population which can live on natural foods and not have to rely on man at all for food. It is best if bears never come near people purposefully. In fact, it is best if bear fear people and intentionally stay away from them. Doing away with hunting activities which do no harm to others, which keep the bear population in check, which result in a safer hunting situation, which result in a stable bear population, and which cause bear to fear people does not seem like the best idea to me.

THE PROBLEM WITH BEARS

FOOD. FOOD. FOOD. FOOD. FOOD.
GARBAGE. GARBAGE. GARBAGE. GARBAGE. GARBAGE.
DON'T FEED THE BEARS.
AND DON'T FORGET IT!

ABOUT THE AUTHOR

David E. Young has worked at Porcupine Mountains Wilderness State Park since 1974, and for several years prior to that worked at Fort Wilkins State Park near Copper Harbor, Michigan. He began working for the Michigan Department of Natural Resources as a Summer Ranger while attending Michigan State University. Majoring in Park and Recreation Resources, he graduated in 1972 with high honors. Dave has also been a Chief Steward for the Michigan State Employees Association since 1980.

In late 1991, Dave published a documentary history of the U. S. Bill of Rights with special emphasis on the intent of the Second Amendment (right to keep and bear arms) after having diligently researched the subject for over twenty years. Dave did all typing, editing and also typesetting of *The Origin of the Second Amendment* himself, just as he did for all three editions of *True Bear Tales*.

Collecting Lake Superior Agate specimens is Dave's favorite hobby. He also enjoys sea kayaking on Lake Superior.

Dave lives in Ontonagon, Michigan with his wife, Arlene, and their four children, Jon, Amy, David, and Tom.

ALSO AVAILABLE FROM GOLDEN OAK BOOKS

The ORIGIN of the SECOND AMENDMENT; A Documentary History of the Bill of Rights in Commentaries on Liberty, Free Government and an Armed Populace 1787-1792
Edited by David E. Young.

This volume is a collection of the original sources illustrating our ancestors' opinions regarding the U.S. Constitution, its defects, and the need to amend it with a Bill of Rights. It contains every available document from the period relating to the interpretation of the Second Amendment.

Second Edition Paperback — 892Pages — 6x9 Size — Acid Free Paper
$29.95 per copy plus $5.00 shipping and handling.
(Michigan residents please add 6% state sales tax.)
Quantity discounts are available.
Send orders and inquiries to:
GOLDEN OAK BOOKS
605 Michigan Street
Ontonagon, Michigan 49953
(906) 884-2961